ColorSense

ColorSense®

Creative Color Combinations for Crafters

Susan Levin

sixth&spring books

sixth&spring books

233 Spring Street • New York, NY 10013

Editorial Director ELAINE SILVERSTEIN	Book Design NANCY SABATO-MARTIN	**Vice President, Publisher** **TRISHA MALCOLM**
Book Division Manager ERICA SMITH	Copy Editor KRISTINA SIGLER	**Production Manager** **DAVID JOINNIDES**
Senior Editor MICHELLE BREDESON	Photo Stylist CHRISTINA BATCH	**Creative Director** **JOE VIOR**
Art Director DIANE LAMPHRON	Bookings Manager RACHAEL STEIN	**President** **ART JOINNIDES**
Associate Art Director SHEENA T. PAUL		

Library of Congress Control Number: 2007937711

ISBN-13: 978-1-933027-29-6
ISBN-10: 1-933027-29-0

Manufactured in China

1 3 5 7 9 10 8 6 4 2

First Edition

PREFACE

I love color. It imparts richness, texture and beauty to everything I see. Dark velvety colors console me when I'm sad. Bright vibrant colors are my co-conspirators when I'm happy. Without color, the world would lose much of its subtlety, intimacy and power.

Color enriches my life and enhances my understanding of the world. But there are times when colors grate on my nerves, jar me from complacency and make me want to hide my eyes. How can it be that I love every color yet I may be disappointed, disturbed or disillusioned when I see certain colors?

It's because sometimes:

I see a color outside my zone of cultural understanding.

I see colors combined in a way that makes me queasy.

I see colors that seem to vibrate in front of my eyes.

That's when I want to say, "I hate that color," but I tell myself, "Don't blame the color. Blame the way it was used."

As I studied and learned more about how and why we respond to color, both physically and psychologically, I also discovered guidelines that have helped me use color successfully in my projects. I wrote this book to share that information with you. The guidelines that you will find in this book don't reflect my cultural understanding or my personal preferences. I'll leave it to you to decide if red is the color of heat and hate, or youth and love. You choose if purple is the color of royalty and riches or people-eaters and Popsicles. You decide which color trends please you in your home, on your body and throughout your life. It all depends on your cultural viewpoint and the \context in which the color is used.

The ColorSense method for choosing colors is based on the scientific principles that are part of an ordered universe. Understanding color combinations and how colors interact will provide you with a structure that will lead you to harmonious and balanced relationships. And after all, isn't that what we all want in our lives?

Enjoy this book and the colorful world around you.

— *Susan Levin*

ACKNOWLEDGMENTS

First and foremost, thanks to Gloria Tracy, my business partner of 12 years and co-inventor of the "Device for Determining Color Combinations," otherwise known as the ColorSense Color Selector. The invention of the color selector was the result of many hours of brainstorming together. We were committed to developing a simple tool that would clearly communicate the color concepts that crafters need to make their projects outstanding. We are continually gratified by the response of so many crafters who have told us how helpful our color selector is. When I decided to write this book to graphically illustrate all the combinations that are represented on the color selector, Gloria was my patient advisor and enthusiastic cheerleader when it seemed like the project would never end. Thanks, Gloria, for being a great business partner and a loyal friend.

I would also like to thank Trisha Malcolm, vice president and publisher of Sixth&Spring Books who looked at my first rough concepts and "got it" immediately. Without her support and confidence, this book might never have come into being. I would also like to thank Elaine Silverstein, editorial director, and Michelle Bredeson, senior editor. Their attention to detail and professionalism have made them a pleasure to work with. Thanks also to Diane Lamphron, art director, for her creative direction. Both Diane and Michelle joined the team midstream, but their knowledge and ability to play catch-up made the transitions smooth. Thanks also to Nancy Sabato-Martin, the book's designer, who took all the pieces and turned them into a complete book. Nancy's patience with my less-than-perfect Illustrator skills was especially appreciated.

I would also like to thank Susie Meach, friend and longtime K1C2 employee, for her proofreading skills and for keeping the office running smoothly while I was preoccupied with this book.

And finally, thanks to my long-suffering husband, Peter, who always encourages and supports me in all my endeavors. He never complains when dinner is late (or missing), when I'm late (or missing), or when I'm grumpy because things just aren't going well. Having a supportive husband who is also your best friend is all any gal could ask for!

CONTENTS

H O W   T O   U S E   T H I S   B O O K

Use this book any way you want to! You may simply want to page through the hundreds of color combinations to find one that works for you. Or you may want to dig in and study the color considerations that shape our responses to color (see page 15). Either way, you will find plenty of inspiration and "Aha!" moments, so when picking colors, you will no longer just rely on your favorites or accept the safe and familiar.

The body of this book is divided into chapters based on time-tested color combinations: complements, triads, analogous and monochromatic combinations, and more (see "The Language of Color" on page 19 if these terms are not yet familiar to you). Each chapter's introduction explains the color relationships that determine that combination and shows you how to use the color wheel to find your own combinations.

If you already have a specific color in mind for your project and are looking for colors to coordinate with it, spend a few minutes reading "How to Use the ColorSense Color Selector" (see page 13). The ColorSense Color Selector included with this book will help you find appealing color combinations that include your inspiration color. Reading this section will also give you a deeper understanding of the concepts used in this book.

How the Chapters Are Organized

Every two-page layout in the color-combination chapters is arranged in the same way to make it easy for you to compare color combinations. To help you find colors quickly, there are tabs showing the color combination represented on the outside margins.

Except for the monochromatic combinations, each left-hand page shows the same color combination in three different values: in the left-hand column, Value 1, tints; in the center column,

Color Guideline

When choosing your own color combinations, take advantage of the intermediate values shown on the ColorSense Color Selector and in the color swatches. These intermediate values will help give your combinations just the right amount of contrast and ensure combinations that have subtlety and sophistication.

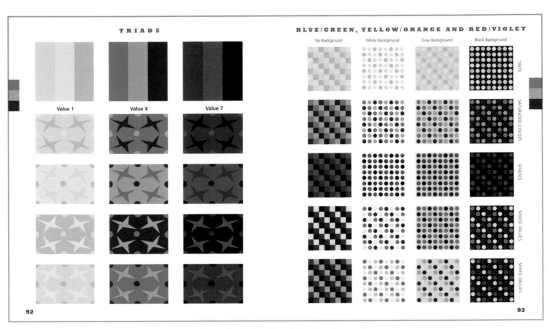

Value 1   Value 4   Value 7

BLUE/GREEN, YELLOW/ORANGE AND RED/VIOLET

No Background | White Background | Gray Background | Black Background

TINTS
SATURATED COLORS
SHADES
MIXED VALUES
MIXED VALUES

93

Sample Color-Combination Layout

Value 4, saturated colors; in the right-hand column, Value 7, shades. At the top of the page, you'll see the colors in three values. Below, you'll see the colors combined in different proportions. When you study these pages, note how radically different the same color combination looks when the dominant color, value or proportion changes.

Each right-hand page shows 20 combinations of the same colors, this time with all colors used in equal proportion. The left-hand column shows the colors without a background. The other three columns show the same colors against white, gray and black backgrounds. The top three rows on each page show tints, saturated colors and shades, respectively. The bottom two rows show combinations of the colors using mixed values. As you look at the page, you can see how dramatically different the color combination looks when the values or background change.

Other Tools
Two other important color tools are included with this book to help you make good color choices. In the back of the book you will find a set of swatches for all the colors found on the ColorSense Color Selector. Cut them out and use them to experiment with color combinations and proportions. (Each swatch has a number and color name on the back to help you identify it.)

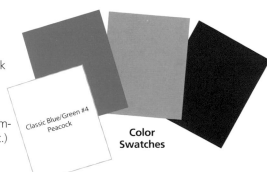

Classic Blue/Green #4
Peacock

Color Swatches

Depending on how you arrange the swatches, you will discover new combinations and get a fresh take on the familiar. Carry them with you when you shop to help keep your chosen combinations in mind.

At the back of the book you will also find masking templates. Cut out the templates and use them to isolate color combinations—this allows you to see the combinations without interference from background colors. You can use the templates with the swatches provided or substitute the actual materials you plan to use for your project. The templates also will help you visualize how a combination looks against different background colors. With the masking templates, the color swatches and the ColorSense Color Selector you have a complete color kit to help you make exciting, creative color choices.

**Masking
Templates**

Categories of Colors

There are many different ways to organize and identify colors. Artists and crafters most often use the Red-Yellow-Blue color identification system. It's the system many of us learned in elementary school. Two other well-known color identification systems are used for printing and electronic technology. They are explained at the bottom of this page. This book uses the Red-Yellow-Blue system, which consists of three categories of colors:

● **Primary** Primary colors are red, yellow and blue. They are called primary colors because they cannot be obtained by mixing other colors. When primary colors are mixed together, a wide range of colors may be created. There are many different natural and manufactured sources for the basic red-yellow-blue colorants. Consequently, there is an almost endless array of color possibilities in fabrics, yarn, ink, paint and other materials.

● **Secondary** When two primary colors are mixed together, they form the secondary colors: blue and red make violet, yellow and blue make green, and red and yellow make orange.

● **Tertiary** When the first six colors are mixed further (one primary color with each adjacent secondary color), the result is the six tertiary colors: blue/violet, red/violet, yellow/green, blue/green, yellow/orange and red/orange.

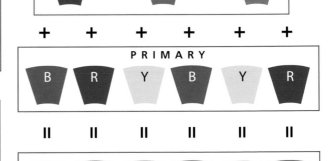

Note: Printers use the CMYK system, based on four ink colors: Cyan (a turquoise blue), Magenta, Yellow and blacK. When these ink colors are mixed in different proportions, they form a wide range of colors suitable for printing on paper.

Computers, televisions and other light-based devices use a method that combines light of three different wavelengths: Red, Green and Blue (RGB). The number and quality of the colors created is influenced by the quality of the screen on which they are viewed.

Adding Black, White or Gray

When black is added to a color, its value is deepened (see chart below). Colors with black added are called **shades**. When white is added to a color, the color's value is lightened. These colors are called **tints**. Finally, to add further distinction, all colors can also be mixed with gray. Colors with gray added are called **tones**.

Classic Colors start with a fully saturated hue that has no black or white added. Increasing amounts of black are added to the starting hue to make shades; increasing amounts of white are added to create tints. On the ColorSense Color Selector, the same amounts of black and white were added to the fully saturated hue in each color family so that the darkness or lightness of each value in all the color families is similar.

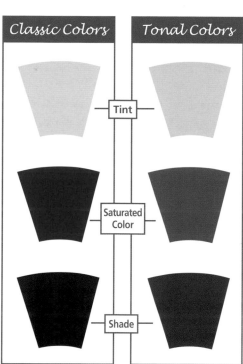

Classic Colors *Tonal Colors*

Tint

Saturated Color

Shade

Tonal Colors begin with a saturated color and its tints and shades (classic colors). Gray that has the same value as the beginning hue is then added to these colors. In the samples shown at left, the tint of red had pale gray added to it. The shade of red had dark gray added to it. Because the grays added had the same values as the classic hues, they were softened, or "toned," without being made darker or lighter.

Color Guideline

Notice that the more colors are mixed, the less vivid they become; however, mixed colors are often considered sophisticated and trendy.

The ColorSense Color Selector is an excellent tool to help you understand the principles of balanced and harmonious color combinations. All color wheels arrange colors based on wavelength: the order in which colors appear in the light spectrum from the shortest wavelength (red) to the longest (violet). When the spectrum is arranged in a circle, it forms a color wheel.

The 12 color families shown on the ColorSense Color Selector include the primary, secondary and tertiary colors. Look on the back of your color selector to see the name of each color family. Each color family includes seven color values ranging from light to dark (tints to shades). The bottom center value (4) is the saturated, or pure, color—no white or black has been added to that color. Values 1–3 are tints. Values 5–7 are shades.

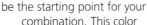

The Red Color Family

ColorSense Color Selector

To use the ColorSense Color Selector, first find your color inspiration. This may be a paint chip, a fabric, a fiber or a favorite family photo—whatever you want to be the starting point for your combination. This color does not have to be the main color in your combination, but it is the one that all the colors you choose should coordinate with.

Place your inspiration piece under each cutout window until you find the best match of color and value. You may not find an exact match for your inspiration color, since your inspiration may be a fashion mix or a grayed tone, but you should be able to associate it with one of the 12 color families. Experiment with two-, three- and four-color combinations by following the example on the next page.

Example: Three-Color Combination Notice that there are two triangles on the inner wheel of the color selector, representing two different types of three-color combinations.

So, if you want a three-color combination and your starting color is green, you have two possible choices. Turn the inner wheel until the starred corner of one of the triangles is pointing to the green color family. The two other corners of the triangle will point to the best choices for other colors in that combination.

If you chose the orange triangle, your combination would be green, red/violet and red/orange.

If you chose the red triangle, your combination would be green, violet and orange.

Now decide which of the seven green values your inspiration color most closely matches and choose the same value for the other colors in your combination. For example, if your inspiration most closely resembles Value 1, a light green tint, consider also making the other colors in your combination light tints. This will ensure a balanced and harmonious combination.

Before settling on the color combination for your project, continue to experiment with the symmetrical shapes on the inner wheel. For example, if you use the square tetrad, your color choices would be green, blue/violet, red and yellow/orange. As the shapes rotate and the combinations change, the relationships between the colors don't change. The consistent spacing, which is based on well-known color principles, ensures pleasing combinations.

The remainder of this book will help you visualize the numerous combinations that you can create by using the ColorSense Color Selector. Each chapter covers color combinations with a different number of colors. As you use the ColorSense Color Selector and this book, you will quickly appreciate how many pleasing and harmonious color combinations you can create.

Color Guideline

Choose colors in natural, slightly shaded light or in the room where you will use the combination. Bright light, either natural or artificial, will distort color perception. If you change the light, you also change the color.

COLOR CONSIDERATIONS

Choosing a color combination is just the first step in completing a project that pleases you and is successful. We have all chosen colors that we love for a project only to find that the outcome didn't measure up to our expectations. By considering the following factors that influence color, you will eliminate many of the challenges you have experienced in the past. Some of these considerations may already be familiar to you, but one of the others just might provide the insight you need to make your next project perfect.

● **Proportion** Projects are usually most pleasing when color and space are not divided equally. Changes in proportion help the viewer focus on the most important elements. There are mathematical formulas and theories about this concept, but a simple guideline summarizes the idea well.

Space and color are most pleasing when they are divided into proportions of one-third and two-thirds. Therefore, if you are working with a three-color combination, mentally divide your project into three parts. The smallest part, representing only about 5% of the total, is for your accent color. The remainder is then divided into one-third (supporting color) and two-thirds (main color). For a four-color combination, reserve about 5% of the total for an accent and divide the remaining space into one-third and two thirds. The two thirds portion is for your main color. Finally, divide the one-third portion again into one-third and two-thirds to create two supporting colors. This guideline is a quick way to visualize color proportion, no matter how many colors your combination includes.

Color Proportions

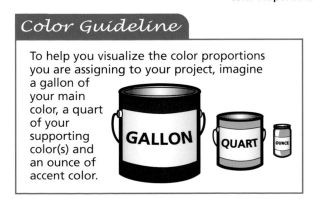

Color Guideline

To help you visualize the color proportions you are assigning to your project, imagine a gallon of your main color, a quart of your supporting color(s) and an ounce of accent color.

GALLON **QUART** OUNCE

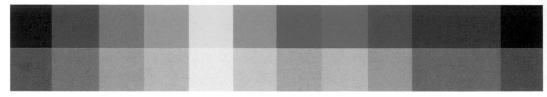

Color Values

● **Value**   Value refers to the lightness or darkness of a color relative to a scale that ranges from white to black (see above). Some colors are by their nature very light, even when they are fully saturated. The illustration shows how the 12 saturated colors on the ColorSense Color Selector compare to a gray scale.

Color value is important when you combine colors, because when colors are placed side by side, lighter colors will appear to come forward and darker colors will appear to recede. To evaluate the relative value of your chosen colors, place them side by side and make black-and-white photocopies of them. You will see immediately which colors are lightest and will be most prominent.

● **Contrast**   The more an object contrasts with its surroundings, the more visible it becomes. Colors with the same value will have little contrast. If they are also analogous (close to each other on the color wheel), they may appear to bleed into each other. This may be desirable if you want to get a smooth flow of color but undesirable if you want to feature an object, pattern or text.

● **Simultaneous Contrast**

When contrasting colors are placed next to each other, their appearance changes. The effect is most intense when complementary colors are placed next to each other. The

This is harder to read.

This is easier to read.

image or text may even appear to vibrate or cast a shadow. Depending on the influence of the surrounding color, the colors may also appear to be warmer or cooler.

A similar effect occurs when a medium color or gray is placed against a dark or a light background. In the example on the right, the medium-gray image appears darker against the light background and lighter against the dark background.

● **Undertones**   The 12 color families and their tints and shades shown on the ColorSense Color Selector were created using the purest, simplest expression of each hue. In the real world, however, almost all colors are more complex, because most materials have undertones of one or more additional colors. This creates rich, complex colors, but it may also make choosing a successful color combination from among the materials available more difficult.

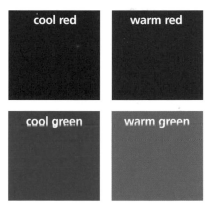

To take account of the effect of undertones, look carefully at the materials you have chosen for your combination. Often undertones are very subtle, but if you look carefully, you will see them. Compare the undertones in the different materials you plan to use. If the undertones don't coordinate, even though the color family is correct, the combination may not be successful. Try to find substitute materials so that all the undertones coordinate.

● **Advancing and Receding Colors**   In general, warm colors and light-value colors appear to advance. Cool colors and dark values tend to recede. Make sure none of your colors recedes or comes forward in an inappropriate area.

● **Echoing Images**   When you are making a project that has a central motif or image, such as a photo, start by identifying one or two inspiration colors from that central motif, and be sure to use those colors in the background. Experiment with tints, shades and tones to decide which colors you want to dominate. If you introduce colors unrelated to the main motif, your project may look spotty or disorganized.

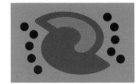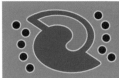

Various Ways of Separating Colors

● **Separation**   The space between your colors is just as important as the colors themselves. So far, we've seen the different effects that can occur when colors are next to each other. When colors are separated by a narrow border or outline, other interesting effects may occur. The dividing lines may throw colors into relief, make colors advance or recede, or blur the division between them. Separation lines give you another interesting way to change your color dynamic, so experiment with them.

● **Toned Palettes**   Sometimes a color combination is too bright for your intended purpose, but you can't find all the materials you need in a toned or muted palette. If some colors in your combination are muted and others are bright, you will get a spotty look. However, there are ways to mute colors so your palette coordinates better. With pens, paints or inks, you may be able to add gray to a color to tone it down. Knitters and spinners may be able to add a fine strand of gray to their chosen yarn or fiber; quilters sometimes tea-dye fabric to get a muted, antique look. Whatever method you use, your project will be more successful if all the colors are from the same palette.

● **Metamers**   Metamers are colors that appear identical under some lighting conditions but not under others. Metamers occur most often when you are working with different materials, such as silk and wool or beads and paint. Different materials reflect light differently, so it is especially important to check mixed media using a variety of light sources.

● **Achromatics, Neutrals and Near-Neutrals**   Black, white and gray are called achromatic because they have no color content. But the lack of color is rarely absolute. Almost all "neutrals" have an undertone that should be taken into consideration when choosing a color combination. Think about how many different white, gray and tan paints, papers and fabrics you can buy. Think about woods that range from the pale yellow of maple to the almost-black of ebony. And don't forget gold and silver. All of these neutrals influence the color of objects around them and in turn will be influenced by colors nearby. Remember to factor neutrals and their influence into your color planning.

THE LANGUAGE OF COLOR

Definitions of the most common terms used to define and identify colors.

Advancing Colors Hues that appear to be nearer or closer to the observer. In general, warm colors and light-value colors tend to advance.

Analogous Colors Hues that are next to each other on the color wheel.

Balance The placement of design elements or the arrangement of colors that produces an aesthetically pleasing composition.

Chroma Synonym for saturation and intensity.

Color What the eye sees when light is reflected off an object. Response to this phenomenon can be influenced by physical, psychological, cultural and language differences. Hue, value and saturation are the terms used to describe different aspects of color.

Colorant A substance that reacts with an object or surface to modify or change its color. Dye and ink colorants are usually transparent; pigments and most paints are generally opaque.

Color Wheel A circular diagram in which colors are arranged sequentially. The arrangement of colors on a color wheel is based on their position in the spectrum of light.

Complements, Complementary Colors Hues directly opposite each other on the color wheel. They heighten or intensify each other when placed next to each other in compositions.

Cool Colors The green-blue-violet range of colors in the spectrum. Cool colors are usually perceived as calm and clean. They tend to recede into the background.

Counterpoints Two-color combinations in which a hue is combined with a second color that is to the right or left of its complement.

Harmony A pleasing combination of elements in a composition.

Hue Another name for color.

Intensity Synonym for chroma and saturation.

Metamers Colors that appear to be identical under some light conditions but not under others.

Monochromatic Containing only one color. A monochromatic color combination may include more- or less-saturated versions of the same color as well as tints or shades of the saturated color.

Neutral Colors Hues with such low saturation that they appear to have little or no color. However, they usually contain an undertone of the base color that makes them appear warm or cool. They are often used as a background for colors of high intensity.

Optical Color Mixing An effect that occurs when small amounts of two different colors, placed side by side, appear to create a third color when viewed from a distance. The color viewed is similar to the color that would result if the original colors were actually mixed together.

Palette A group of colors used by an artist or designer in a specific work of art.

Primary Colors Hues from which all others can be produced: red, yellow and blue.

Pure Color Synonym for saturated color.

Receding Colors Hues that appear to move away, or recede from, the viewer. In general, cool colors and dark-value colors tend to recede.

Saturation The relative purity or strength of a color. A fully saturated color is at its most intense (Value 4 of each hue on the ColorSense Color Selector). When a color is mixed with black, gray, white or its complement, it becomes less saturated. Synonyms include chroma and intensity.

Secondary Colors Hues formed by combining two primary colors: orange, green and violet.

Shade A saturated color mixed with black.

Spectrum The full range of visible colors. A rainbow is an example of a naturally occurring spectrum of colors.

Split Complement A combination consisting of a color plus the two colors on either side of the starting color's complement.

Tertiary Color A hue created by mixing a primary color with an adjacent secondary color. Red/violet, red/orange, yellow/orange, yellow/green, blue/green and blue/violet are all tertiary colors.

Tetrad Two pairs of complements.

Tint A saturated color plus white.

Tone A color plus gray.

Triad Three colors equidistant from each other on a color wheel.

Value The lightness or darkness of a color or gray relative to black or white.

Warm Colors Hues in the red-orange-yellow color range. They are usually perceived as being warm and exciting. They tend to come forward toward the viewer.

CHAPTER 1
Monochromatic Combinations

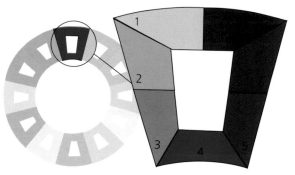

Seven Values of One Color Family

One-color, or monochromatic, combinations use a variety of hues from a single color family. This may include a wide range of tints, tones and shades.

One of the challenges when using a monochromatic combination is defining a focal point. This is especially important for home décor and paper crafts. To create a focal point, choose one value to be your main color. Use your other chosen values for accent colors.

Since monochromatic combinations rely on subtle changes in value to create a mood, they can be boring if the colors are not used creatively. So, in addition to choosing one value as a focal point, use a large variety of media to create interesting texture and patterns. This will give your project a stronger presence. Monochromatic combinations can be elegant or soothing (imagine many shades of blue), dramatic and overwhelming (all pinks and reds) or any other mood.

Value 1	Value 4	Value 7

RED

No Background   White Background   Gray Background   Black Background

MIXED VALUES

MIXED VALUES

MIXED VALUES

MIXED VALUES

MIXED VALUES

Value 1	Value 4	Value 7

RED / ORANGE

No Background	White Background	Gray Background	Black Background	
				MIXED VALUES
				MIXED VALUES
				MIXED VALUES
				MIXED VALUES
				MIXED VALUES

27

MONOCHROMATIC COMBINATIONS

Value 1	Value 4	Value 7

ORANGE

No Background | White Background | Gray Background | Black Background

MIXED VALUES

MIXED VALUES

MIXED VALUES

MIXED VALUES

MIXED VALUES

Value 1	Value 4	Value 7

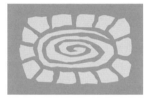   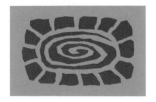

YELLOW/ORANGE

No Background	White Background	Gray Background	Black Background	
				MIXED VALUES
				MIXED VALUES
				MIXED VALUES
				MIXED VALUES
				MIXED VALUES

MONOCHROMATIC COMBINATIONS

Value 1	Value 4	Value 7

 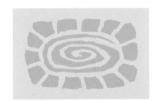 

YELLOW

No Background   White Background   Gray Background   Black Background

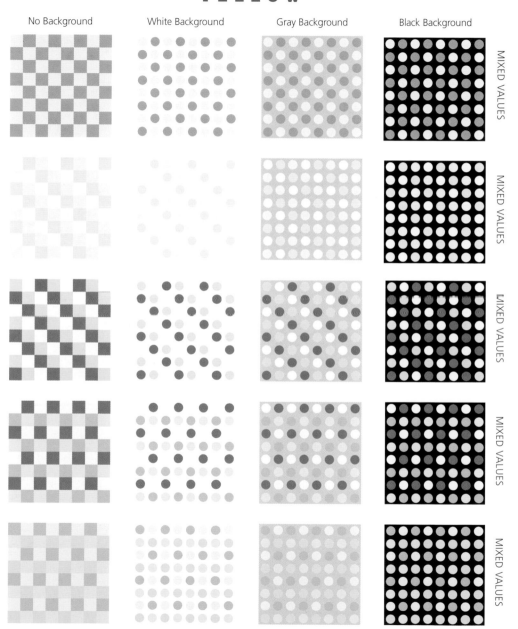

MIXED VALUES

MIXED VALUES

MIXED VALUES

MIXED VALUES

MIXED VALUES

Value 1	Value 4	Value 7

YELLOW / GREEN

No Background   White Background   Gray Background   Black Background

MIXED VALUES

MIXED VALUES

MIXED VALUES

MIXED VALUES

MIXED VALUES

MONOCHROMATIC COMBINATIONS

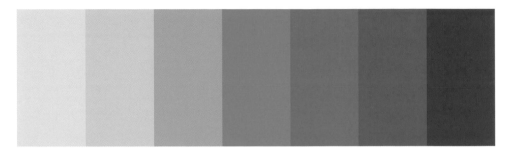

Value 1

Value 4

Value 7

GREEN

No Background White Background Gray Background Black Background

MIXED VALUES

MIXED VALUES

MIXED VALUES

MIXED VALUES

MIXED VALUES

MONOCHROMATIC COMBINATIONS

Value 1	Value 4	Value 7

No Background	White Background	Gray Background	Black Background	
				MIXED VALUES
				MIXED VALUES
				MIXED VALUES
				MIXED VALUES
				MIXED VALUES

Value 1	Value 4	Value 7

BLUE

No Background   White Background   Gray Background   Black Background

MIXED VALUES

MIXED VALUES

MIXED VALUES

MIXED VALUES

MIXED VALUES

Value 1	Value 4	Value 7

BLUE / VIOLET

No Background	White Background	Gray Background	Black Background	
				MIXED VALUES
				MIXED VALUES
				MIXED VALUES
				MIXED VALUES
				MIXED VALUES

Value 1	Value 4	Value 7

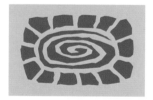  

No Background   White Background   Gray Background   Black Background

MIXED VALUES

MIXED VALUES

MIXED VALUES

MIXED VALUES

MIXED VALUES

Value 1	Value 4	Value 7

No Background	White Background	Gray Background	Black Background	
				MIXED VALUES
				MIXED VALUES
				MIXED VALUES
				MIXED VALUES
				MIXED VALUES

Two-Color Combinations

Complements are located directly opposite each other on the color wheel. The complement of a primary color will always be a secondary color, and vice versa. The complement of a tertiary color will always be another tertiary color.

Complementary color combinations have the highest contrast of any combination and will draw maximum attention to a project. When placed next to each other, complementary colors look vibrant and may even seem to shimmer. To moderate this effect and prevent the two colors from competing, use one color as your main color and the other as an accent. To soften the contrast, try combinations with different values of each color and avoid using same-value complementary colors as a text/background combination, unless you separate them with a neutral color or outline.

Counterpoints are similar to complements, but instead of using colors directly opposite each other as in complementary combinations, counterpoint combinations use the color to the right or left of the complement. This means that a counterpoint combination will always include a tertiary color (for example, red and blue/green). The result will be more unexpected and assertive than a complementary combination. (Counterpoint combinations do not have a special symbol on the ColorSense Color Selector.)

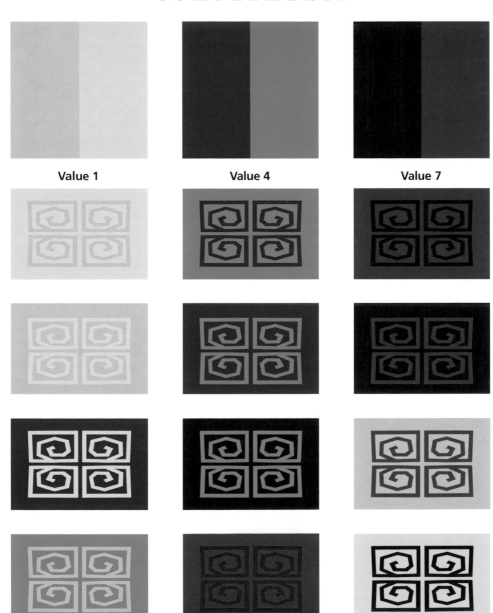

Value 1   Value 4   Value 7

RED AND GREEN

No Background   White Background   Gray Background   Black Background

TINTS

SATURATED COLORS

SHADES

MIXED VALUES

MIXED VALUES

COMPLEMENTS

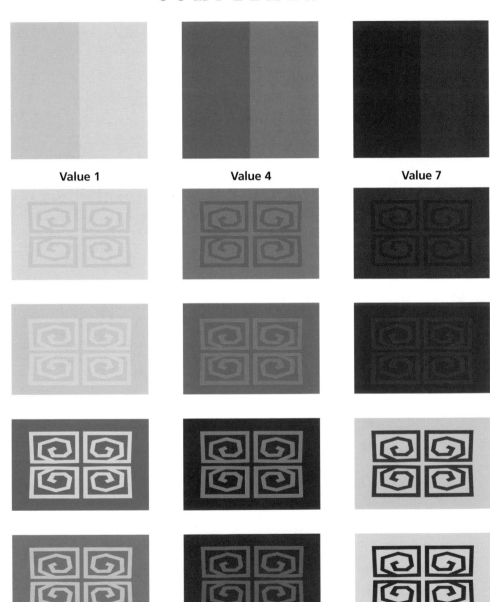

Value 1   Value 4   Value 7

No Background   White Background   Gray Background   Black Background

TINTS

SATURATED COLORS

SHADES

MIXED VALUES

MIXED VALUES

COMPLEMENTS

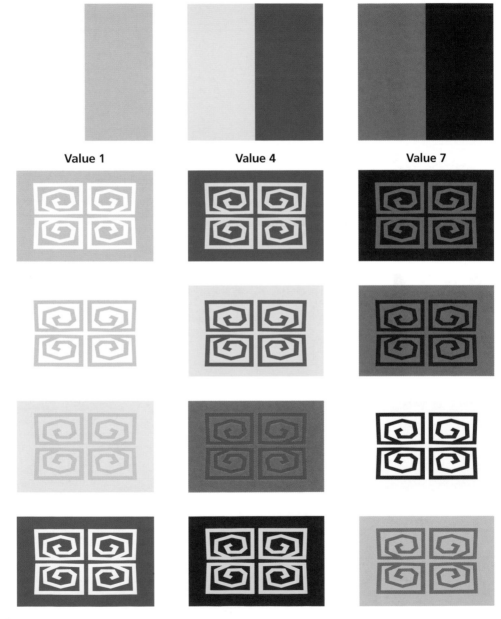

Value 1   Value 4   Value 7

No Background	White Background	Gray Background	Black Background	
				TINTS
				SATURATED COLORS
				SHADES
				MIXED VALUES
				MIXED VALUES

COMPLEMENTS

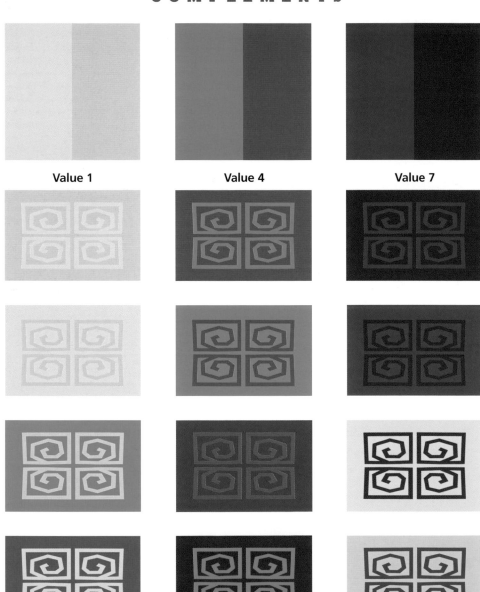

Value 1   Value 4   Value 7

56

BLUE/GREEN AND RED/ORANGE

No Background	White Background	Gray Background	Black Background	

TINTS

SATURATED COLORS

SHADES

MIXED VALUES

MIXED VALUES

COMPLEMENTS

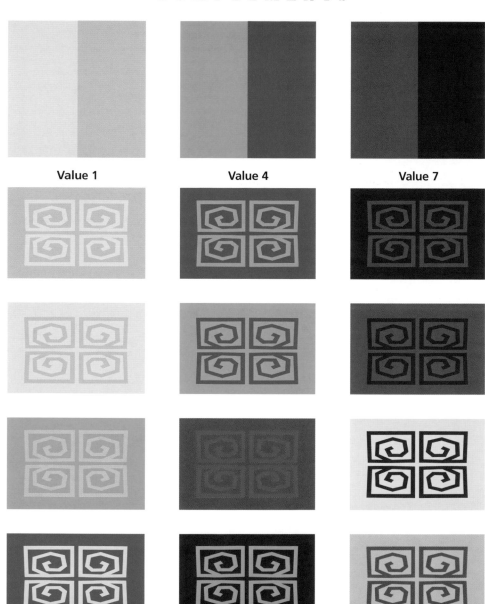

Value 1   Value 4   Value 7

YELLOW/ORANGE AND BLUE/VIOLET

No Background	White Background	Gray Background	Black Background	

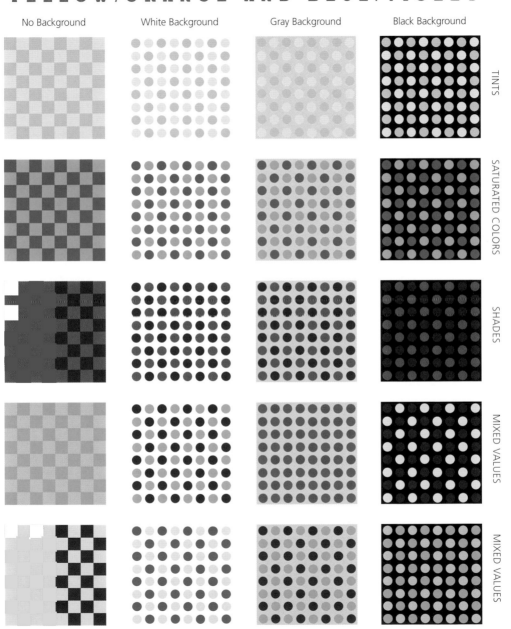

TINTS

SATURATED COLORS

SHADES

MIXED VALUES

MIXED VALUES

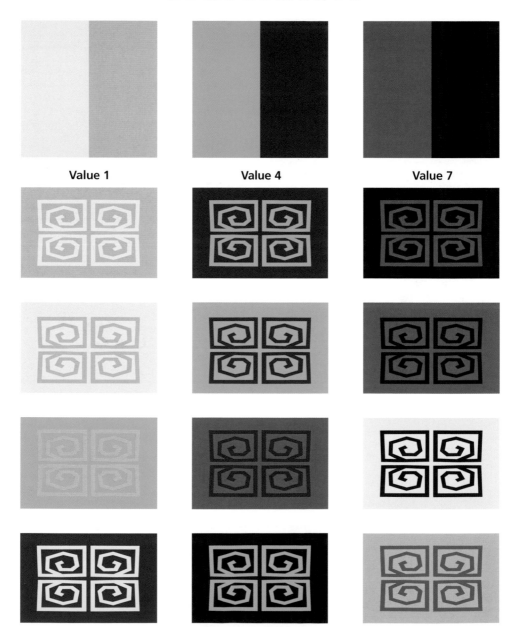

Value 1 Value 4 Value 7

YELLOW/GREEN AND RED/VIOLET

No Background
White Background
Gray Background
Black Background
TINTS
SATURATED COLORS
SHADES
MIXED VALUES
MIXED VALUES

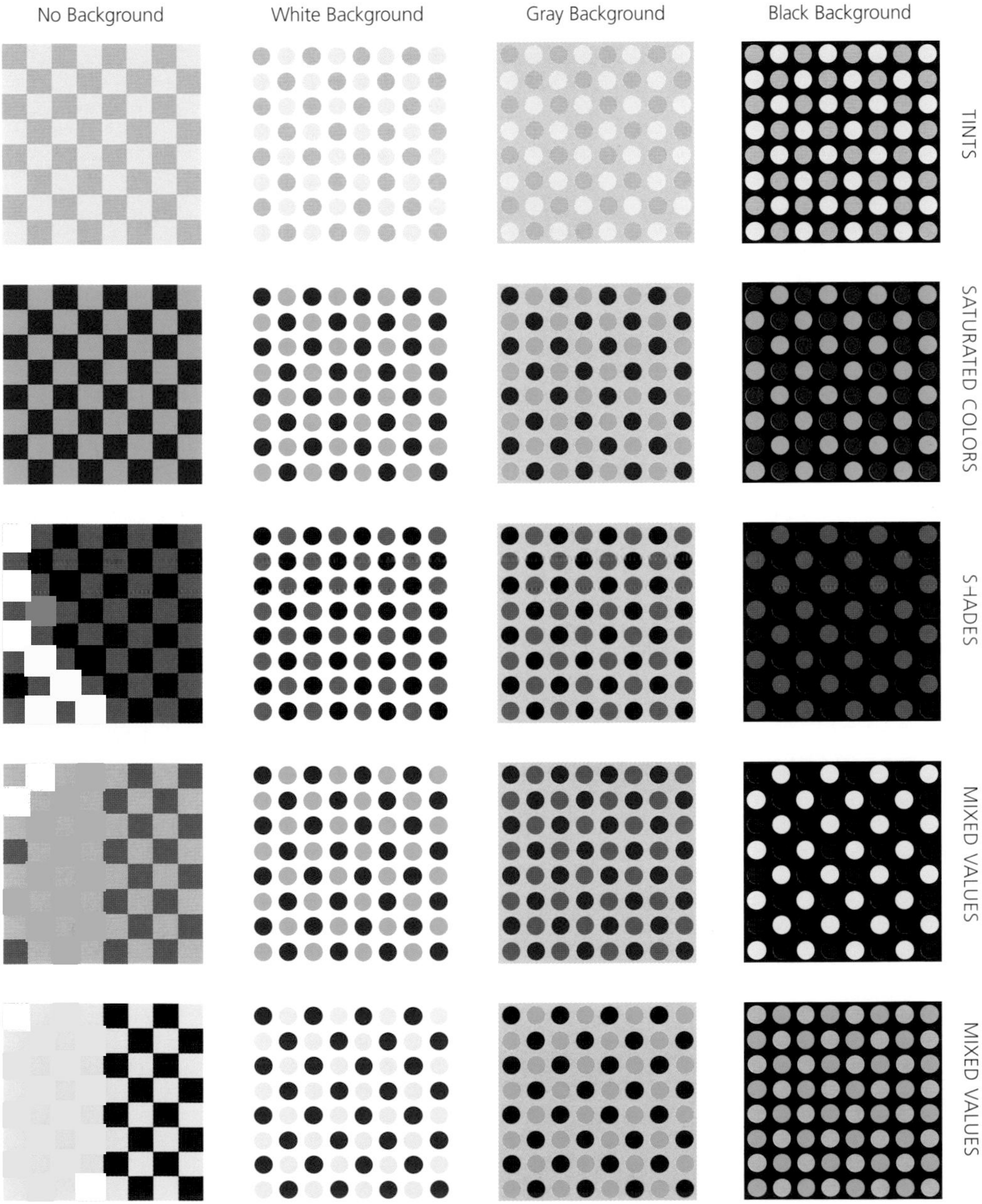

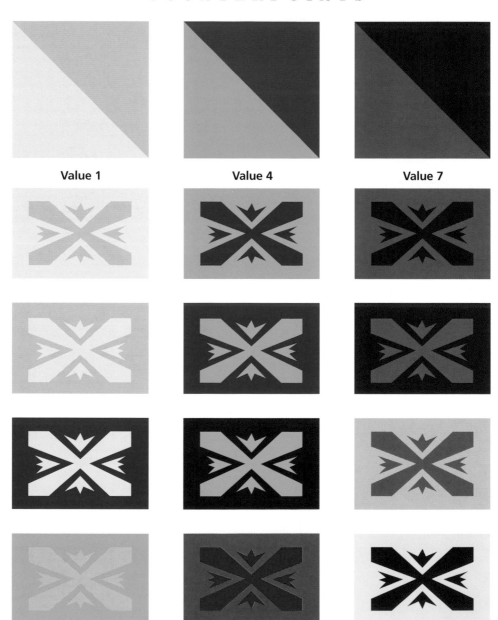

Value 1   Value 4   Value 7

RED AND YELLOW/GREEN

No Background	White Background	Gray Background	Black Background	
				TINTS
				SATURATED COLORS
				SHADES
				MIXED VALUES
				MIXED VALUES

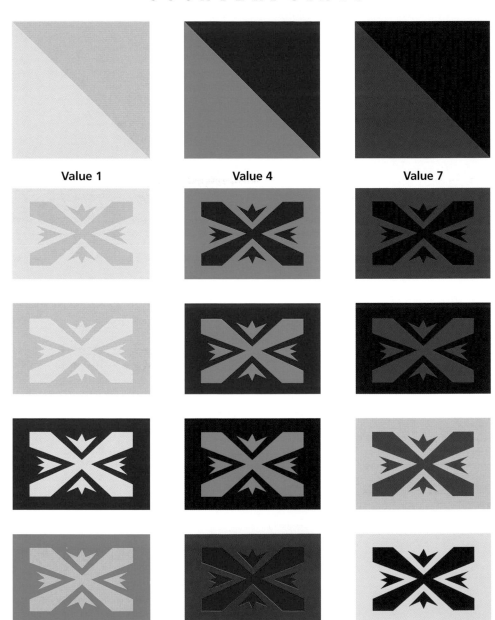

Value 1   Value 4   Value 7

RED AND BLUE/GREEN

No Background	White Background	Gray Background	Black Background	

TINTS

SATURATED COLORS

SHADES

MIXED VALUES

MIXED VALUES

Value 1   Value 4   Value 7

ORANGE AND BLUE/GREEN

No Background	White Background	Gray Background	Black Background	
				TINTS
				SATURATED COLORS
				SHADES
				MIXED VALUES
				MIXED VALUES

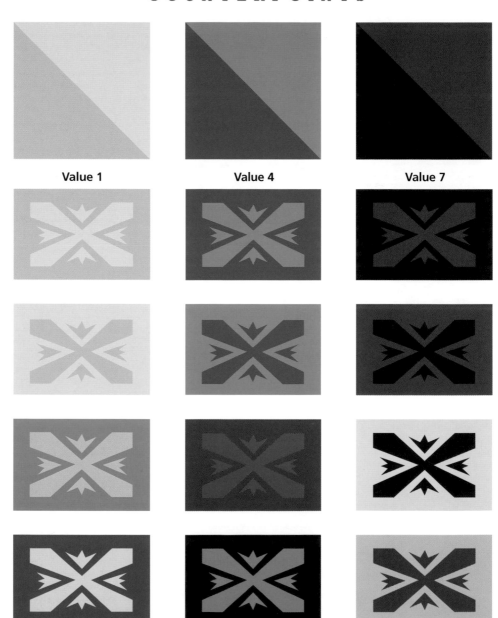

Value 1   Value 4   Value 7

ORANGE AND BLUE/VIOLET

No Background   White Background   Gray Background   Black Background

TINTS

SATURATED COLORS

SHADES

MIXED VALUES

MIXED VALUES

69

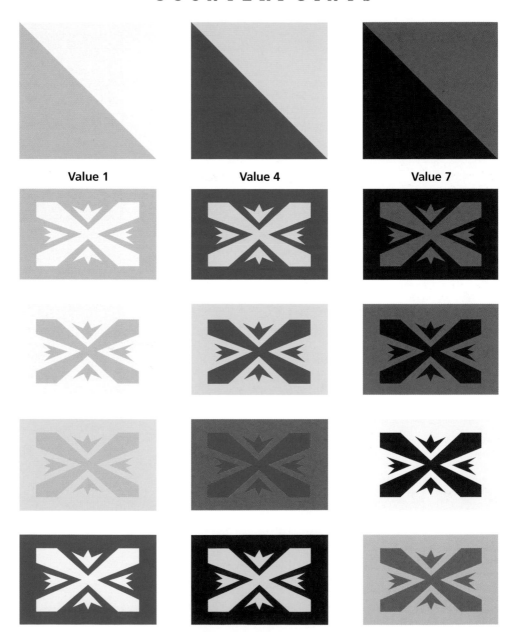

Value 1　　　Value 4　　　Value 7

No Background　　　White Background　　　Gray Background　　　Black Background

TINTS

SATURATED COLORS

SHADES

MIXED VALUES

MIXED VALUES

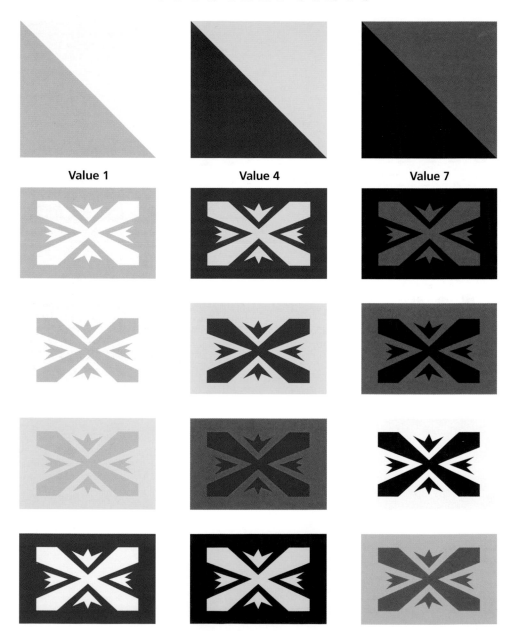

Value 1　　　　Value 4　　　　Value 7

No Background	White Background	Gray Background	Black Background	

TINTS

SATURATED COLORS

SHADES

MIXED VALUES

MIXED VALUES

COUNTERPOINTS

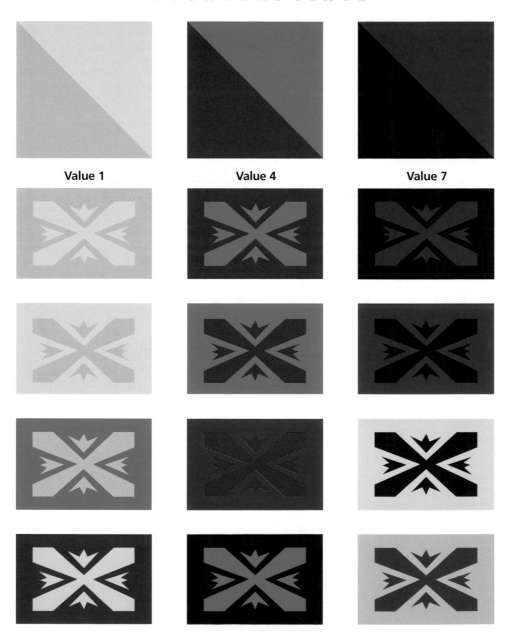

Value 1   Value 4   Value 7

No Background	White Background	Gray Background	Black Background	
				TINTS
				SATURATED COLORS
				SHADES
				MIXED VALUES
				MIXED VALUES

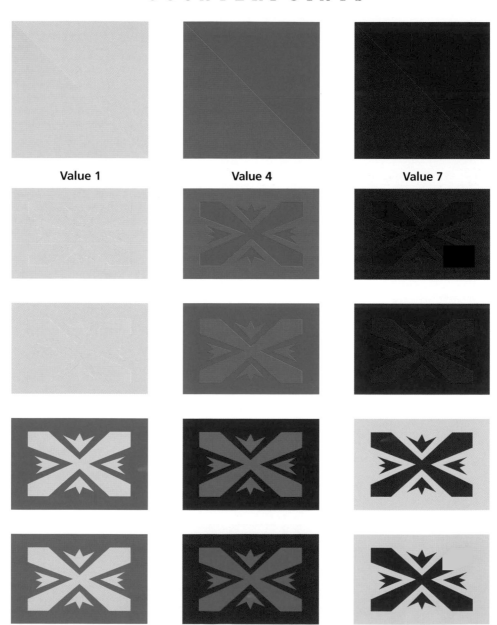

Value 1   Value 4   Value 7

No Background	White Background	Gray Background	Black Background	
				TINTS
				SATURATED COLORS
				SHADES
				MIXED VALUES
				MIXED VALUES

Value 1   Value 4   Value 7

No Background   White Background   Gray Background   Black Background

TINTS

SATURATED COLORS

SHADES

MIXED VALUES

MIXED VALUES

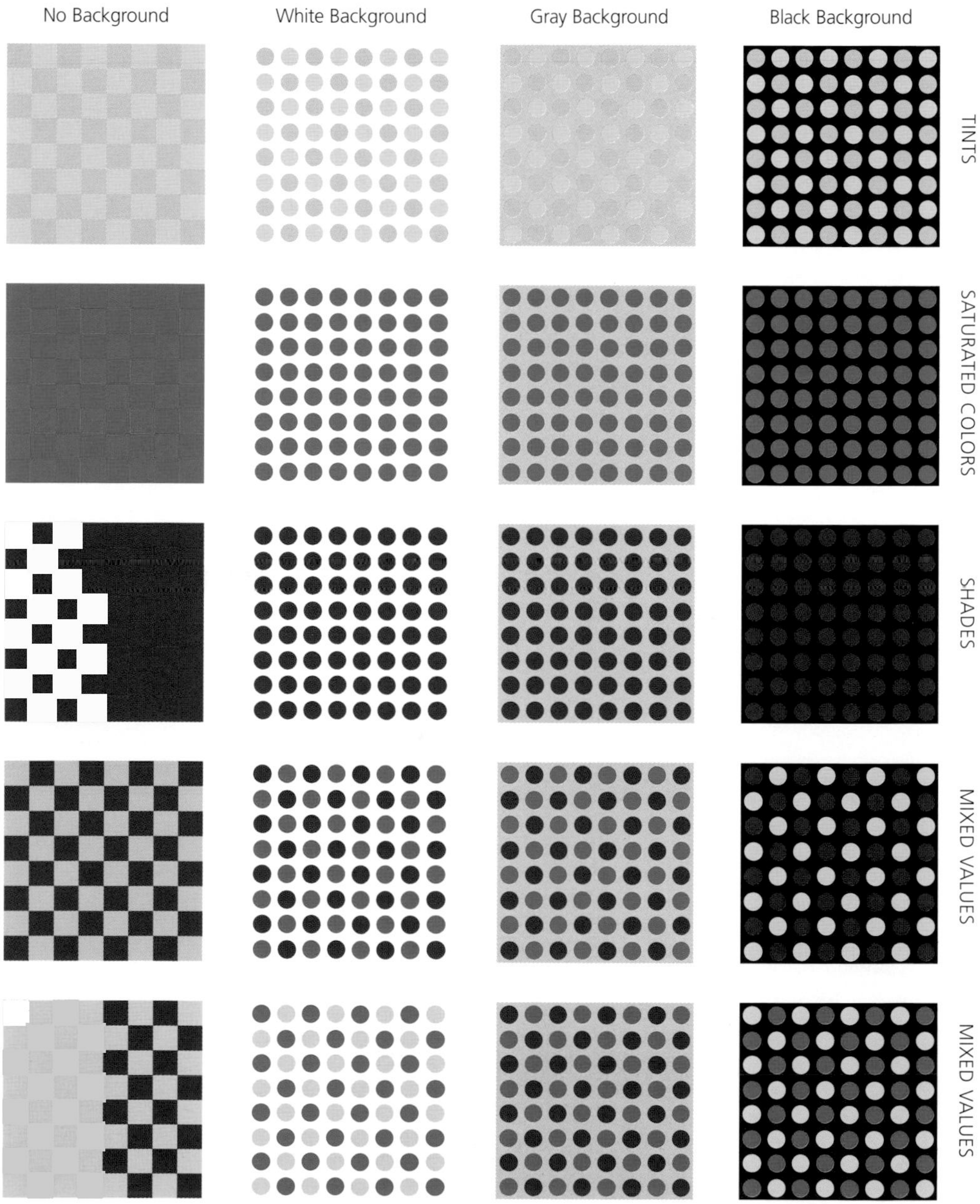

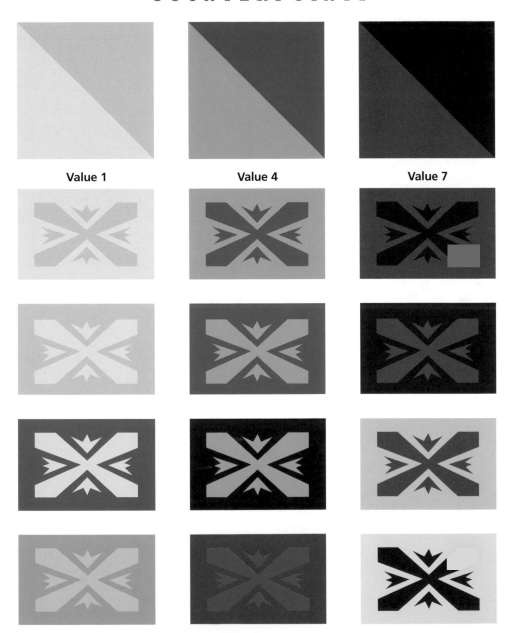

Value 1   Value 4   Value 7

No Background	White Background	Gray Background	Black Background

TINTS

SATURATED COLORS

SHADES

MIXED VALUES

MIXED VALUES

Value 1 Value 4 Value 7

VIOLET AND YELLOW/ORANGE

No Background	White Background	Gray Background	Black Background

TINTS

SATURATED COLORS

SHADES

MIXED VALUES

MIXED VALUES

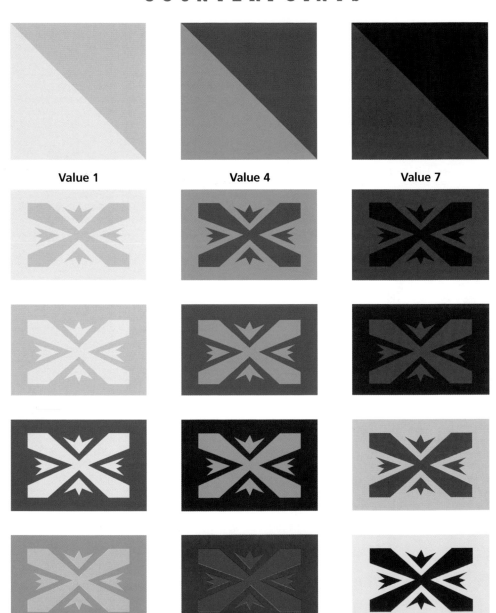

Value 1   Value 4   Value 7

VIOLET AND YELLOW/GREEN

No Background	White Background	Gray Background	Black Background

TINTS

SATURATED COLORS

SHADES

MIXED VALUES

MIXED VALUES

Three-Color Combinations

Triads include three colors that are equally spaced around the color wheel. Triads create balanced color combinations with strong contrast but without the visual intensity of complementary colors. Use the red triangle on the inner wheel of the ColorSense Color Selector to find triads. Triads tend to be vivid and, at times, may appear gaudy. To take advantage of their vibrancy while creating clever and sophisticated combinations, be sure to balance the proportion of each color used and consider varying values.

Split Complements are composed of a color plus the two colors on either side of the complement. These combinations have strong visual contrast, like complements, but they have a lower level of tension because the colors are not in direct opposition. Split complements also have more complexity, as at least one of the colors is always a tertiary color. Use the orange triangle on the inner wheel of the ColorSense Color Selector to find split complements. A split complement is a good choice if you want to emphasize the warmth or coolness of your combination.

Analogous Combinations are made up of three or more colors that are adjacent to each other on the color wheel. Analogous combinations are related to monochromatic combinations but often look richer and more nuanced. If you select analogous colors, you are sure to come up with a beautiful, subtle and harmonious combination.

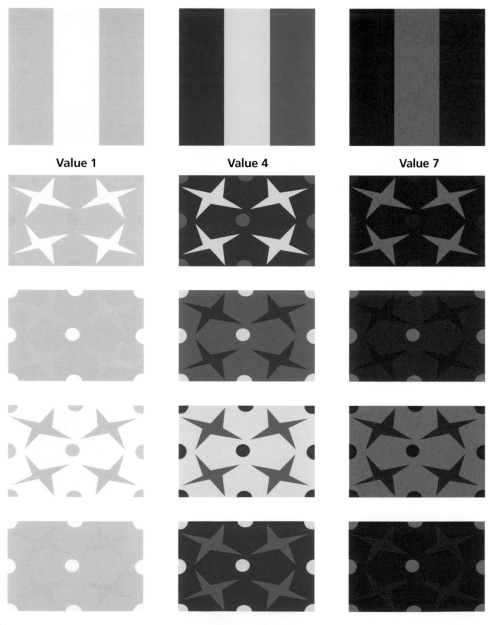

Value 1   Value 4   Value 7

RED, YELLOW AND BLUE

No Background	White Background	Gray Background	Black Background	

TINTS

SATURATED COLORS

SHADES

MIXED VALUES

MIXED VALUES

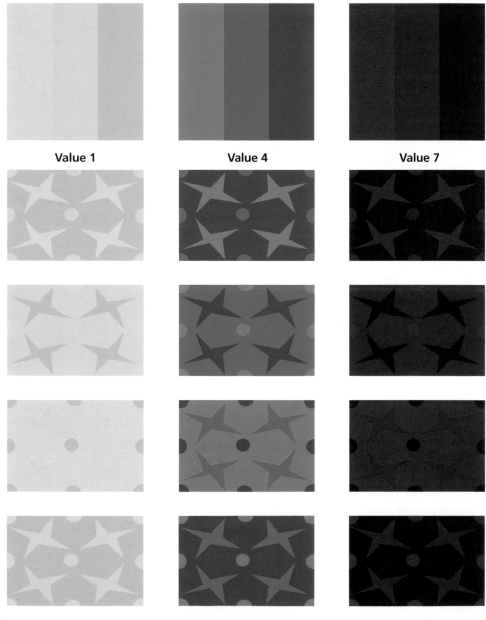

Value 1

Value 4

Value 7

VIOLET, GREEN AND ORANGE

No Background	White Background	Gray Background	Black Background	
				TINTS
				SATURATED COLORS
				SHADES
				MIXED VALUES
				MIXED VALUES

TRIADS

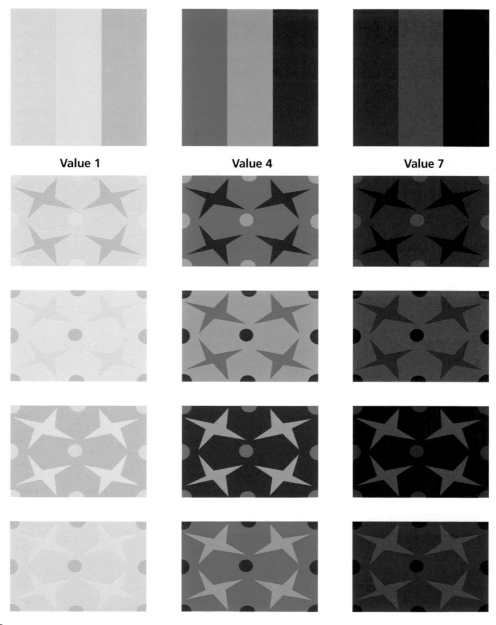

Value 1   Value 4   Value 7

BLUE/GREEN, YELLOW/ORANGE AND RED/VIOLET

No Background	White Background	Gray Background	Black Background	

TINTS

SATURATED COLORS

SHADES

MIXED VALUES

MIXED VALUES

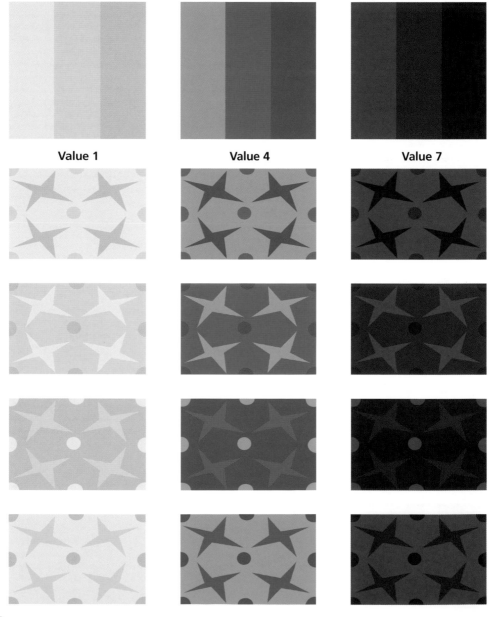

Value 1   Value 4   Value 7

YELLOW/GREEN, RED/ORANGE AND BLUE/VIOLET

No Background	White Background	Gray Background	Black Background	

TINTS

SATURATED COLORS

SHADES

MIXED VALUES

MIXED VALUES

SPLIT COMPLEMENTS

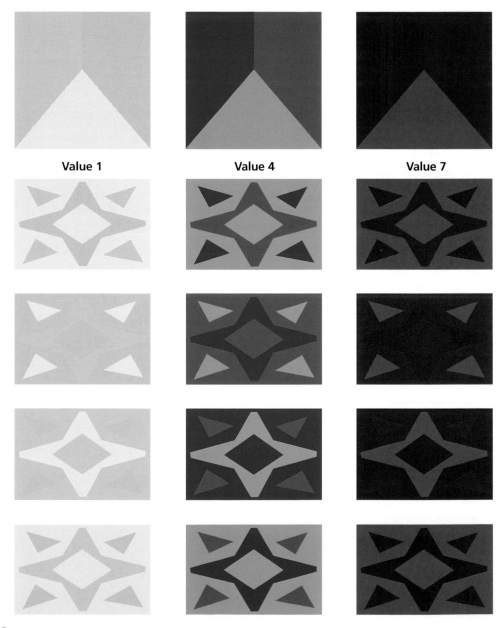

Value 1 Value 4 Value 7

RED, YELLOW/GREEN AND VIOLET

No Background	White Background	Gray Background	Black Background	
				TINTS
				SATURATED COLORS
				SHADES
				MIXED VALUES
				MIXED VALUES

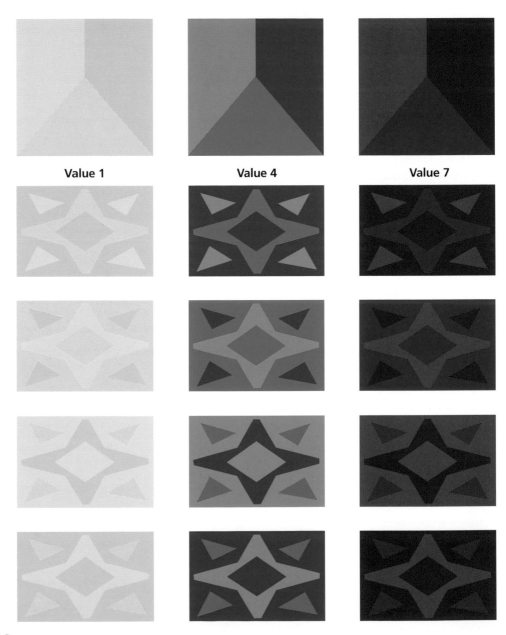

Value 1   Value 4   Value 7

ORANGE, BLUE/GREEN AND RED

No Background	White Background	Gray Background	Black Background	

TINTS

SATURATED COLORS

SHADES

MIXED VALUES

MIXED VALUES

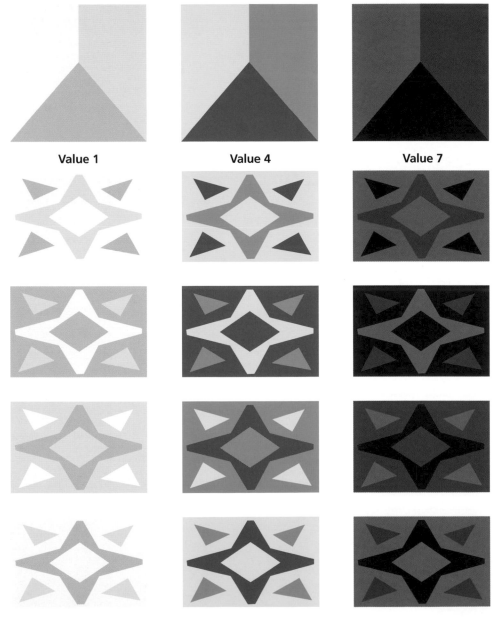

Value 1   Value 4   Value 7

YELLOW, BLUE/VIOLET AND ORANGE

No Background White Background Gray Background Black Background

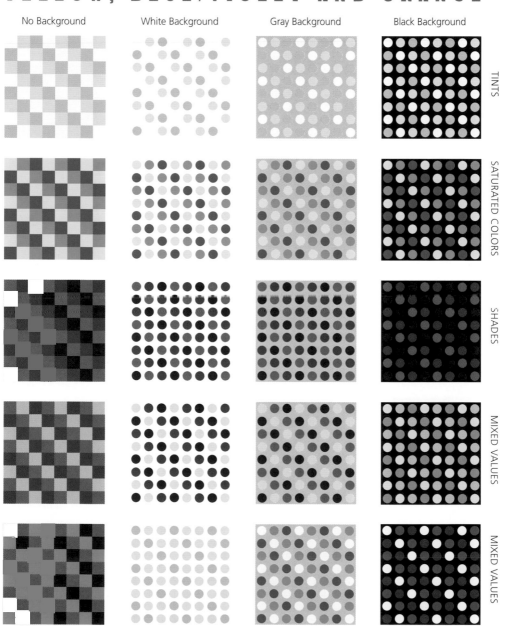

TINTS

SATURATED COLORS

SHADES

MIXED VALUES

MIXED VALUES

SPLIT COMPLEMENTS

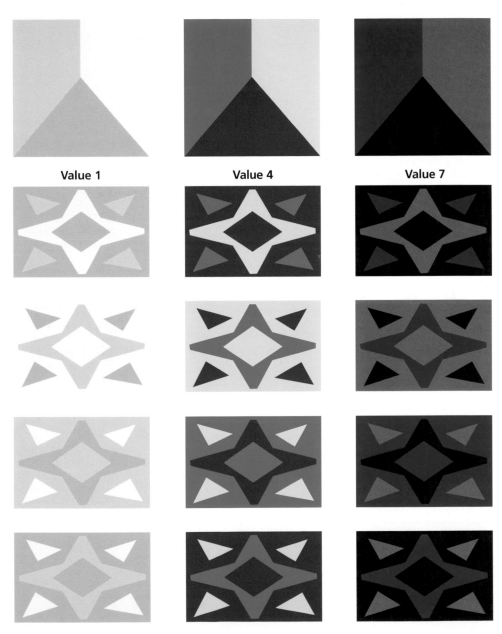

Value 1   Value 4   Value 7

GREEN, RED/VIOLET AND YELLOW

No Background	White Background	Gray Background	Black Background	
				TINTS
				SATURATED COLORS
				SHADES
				MIXED VALUES
				MIXED VALUES

SPLIT COMPLEMENTS

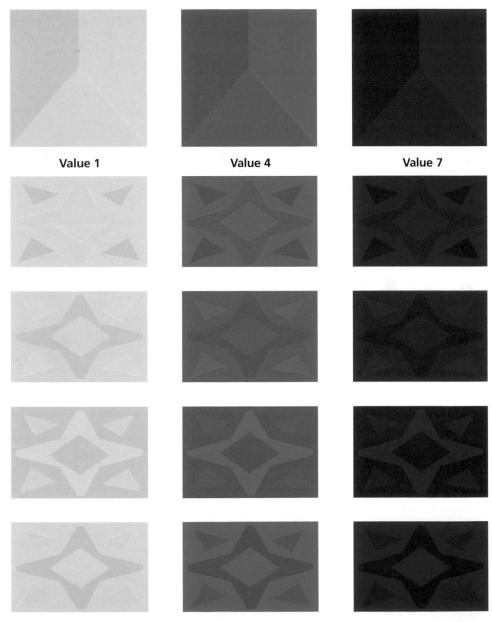

Value 1   Value 4   Value 7

BLUE, RED/ORANGE AND GREEN

No Background	White Background	Gray Background	Black Background	
				TINTS
				SATURATED COLORS
				SHADES
				MIXED VALUES
				MIXED VALUES

SPLIT COMPLEMENTS

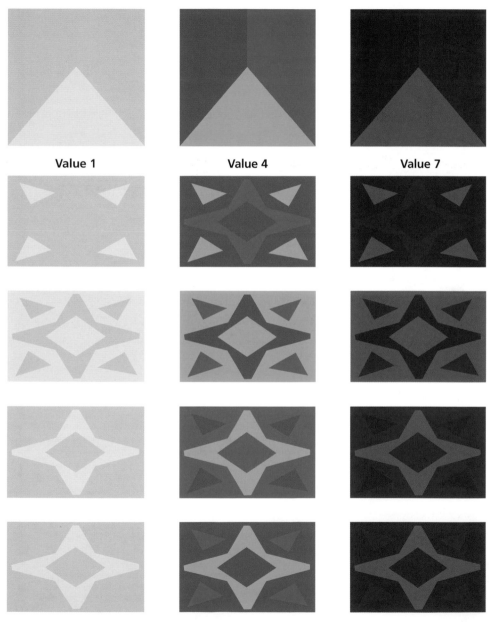

Value 1   Value 4   Value 7

VIOLET, YELLOW/ORANGE AND BLUE

No Background   White Background   Gray Background   Black Background

TINTS

SATURATED COLORS

SHADES

MIXED VALUES

MIXED VALUES

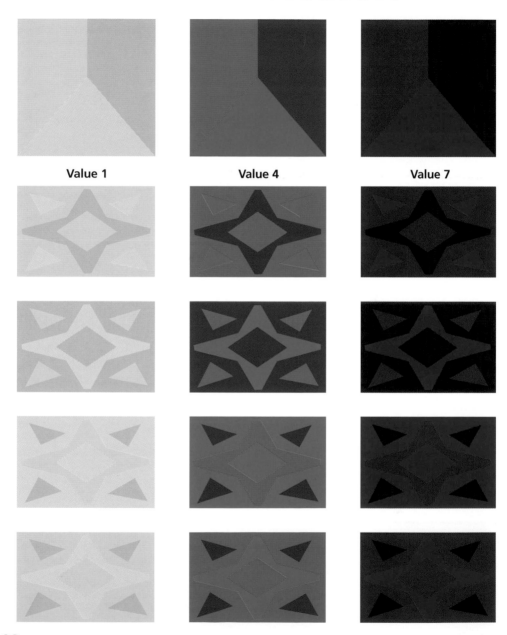

Value 1 Value 4 Value 7

RED / ORANGE, GREEN AND RED / VIOLET

No Background   White Background   Gray Background   Black Background

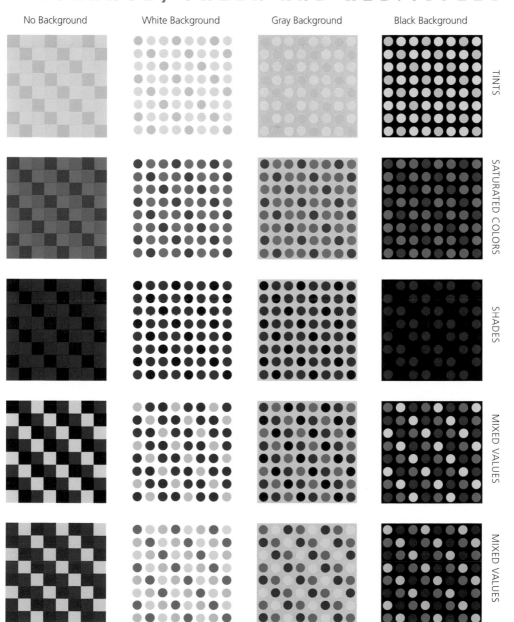

TINTS

SATURATED COLORS

SHADES

MIXED VALUES

MIXED VALUES

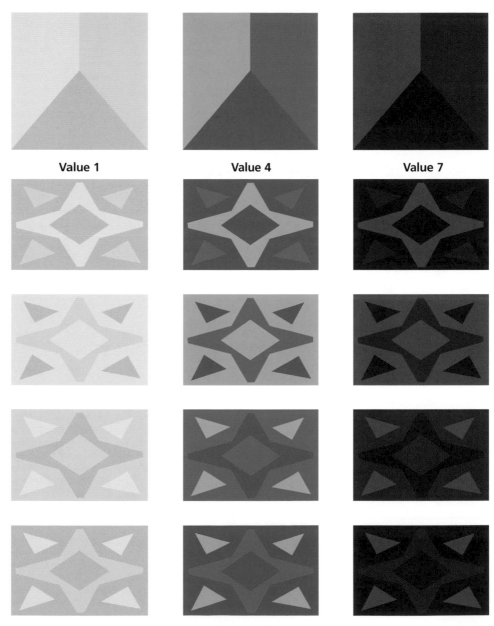

Value 1   Value 4   Value 7

YELLOW/ORANGE, BLUE AND RED/ORANGE

No Background   White Background   Gray Background   Black Background

TINTS

SATURATED COLORS

SHADES

MIXED VALUES

MIXED VALUES

SPLIT COMPLEMENTS

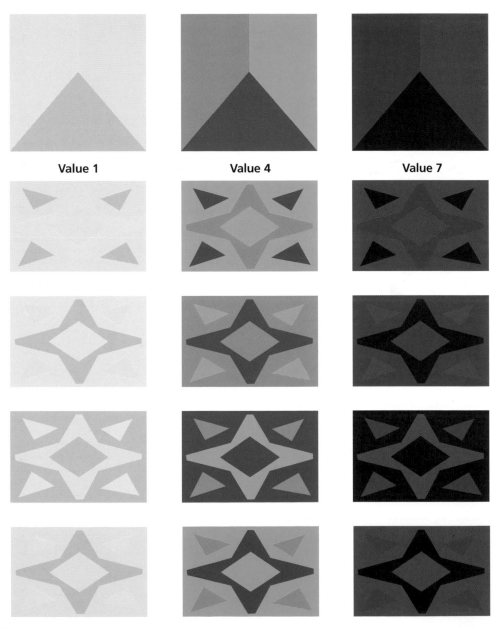

Value 1   Value 4   Value 7

No Background	White Background	Gray Background	Black Background	
				TINTS
				SATURATED COLORS
				SHADES
				MIXED VALUES
				MIXED VALUES

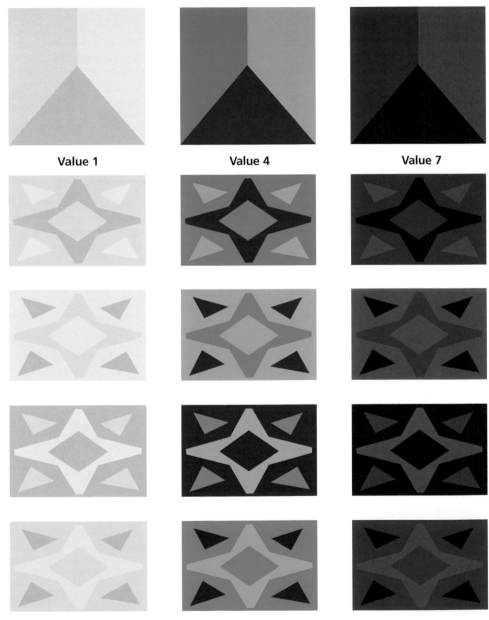

Value 1   Value 4   Value 7

No Background	White Background	Gray Background	Black Background	
				TINTS
				SATURATED COLORS
				SHADES
				MIXED VALUES
				MIXED VALUES

SPLIT COMPLEMENTS

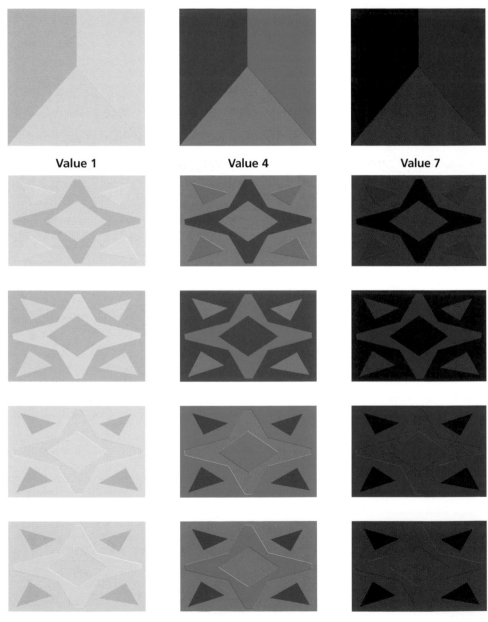

Value 1   Value 4   Value 7

BLUE/VIOLET, ORANGE AND BLUE/GREEN

No Background	White Background	Gray Background	Black Background	

TINTS

SATURATED COLORS

SHADES

MIXED VALUES

MIXED VALUES

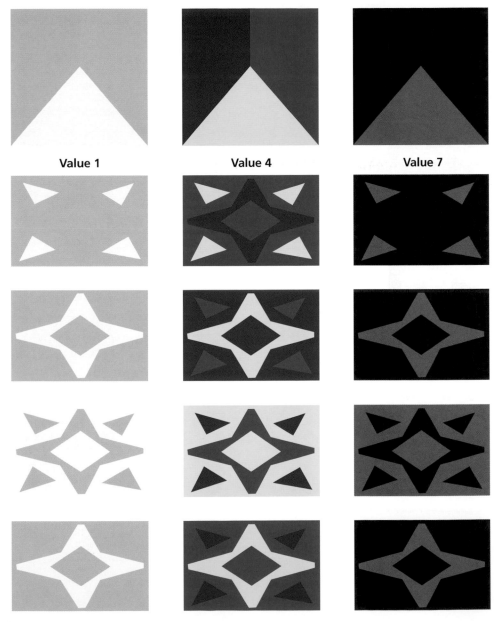

Value 1   Value 4   Value 7

No Background   White Background   Gray Background   Black Background

TINTS

SATURATED COLORS

SHADES

MIXED VALUES

MIXED VALUES

ANALOGOUS COMBINATIONS

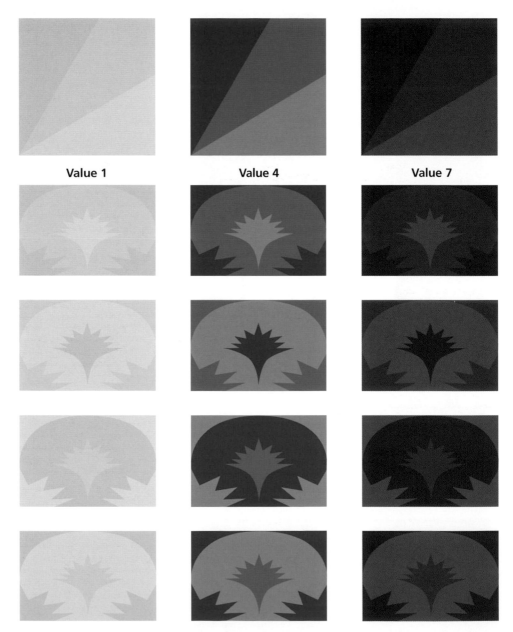

Value 1 Value 4 Value 7

No Background	White Background	Gray Background	Black Background	
				TINTS
				SATURATED COLORS
				SHADES
				MIXED VALUES
				MIXED VALUES

ANALOGOUS COMBINATIONS

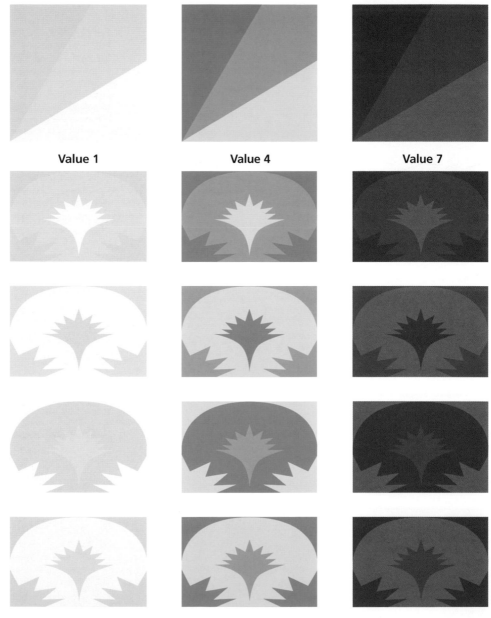

Value 1   Value 4   Value 7

ORANGE, YELLOW/ORANGE AND YELLOW

No Background   White Background   Gray Background   Black Background

TINTS

SATURATED COLORS

SHADES

MIXED VALUES

MIXED VALUES

ANALOGOUS COMBINATIONS

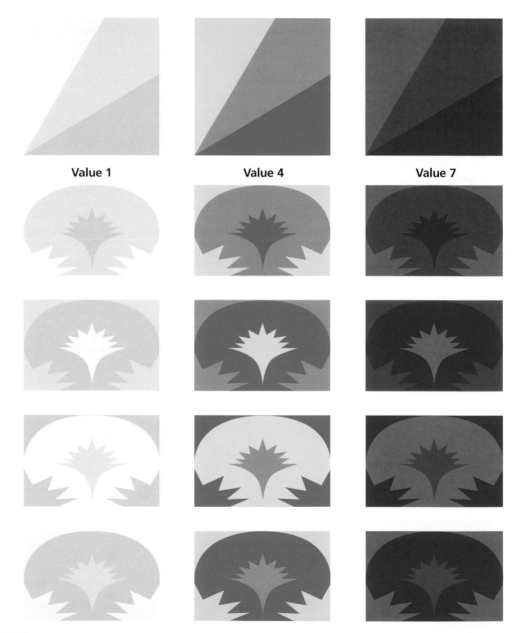

Value 1   Value 4   Value 7

YELLOW, YELLOW/GREEN AND GREEN

No Background   White Background   Gray Background   Black Background

TINTS

SATURATED COLORS

SHADES

MIXED VALUES

MIXED VALUES

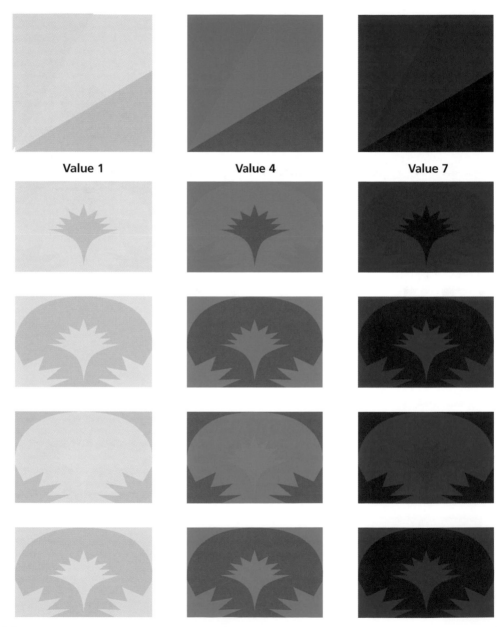

Value 1   Value 4   Value 7

GREEN, BLUE/GREEN AND BLUE

No Background | White Background | Gray Background | Black Background

TINTS

SATURATED COLORS

SHADES

MIXED VALUES

MIXED VALUES

ANALOGOUS COMBINATIONS

Value 1   Value 4   Value 7

BLUE, BLUE/VIOLET AND VIOLET

No Background   White Background   Gray Background   Black Background

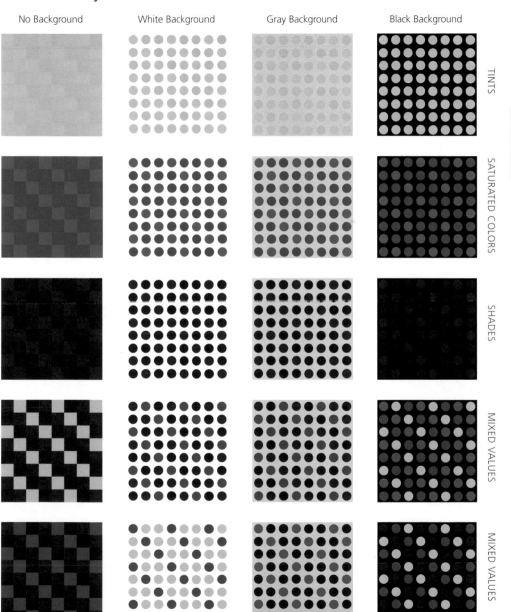

TINTS

SATURATED COLORS

SHADES

MIXED VALUES

MIXED VALUES

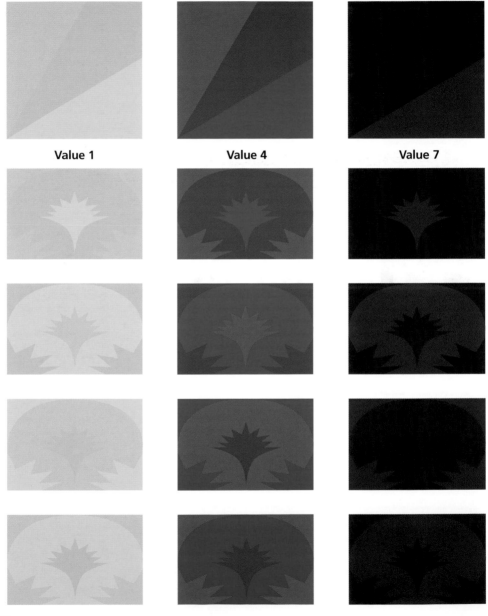

Value 1   Value 4   Value 7

VIOLET, RED/VIOLET AND RED

No Background	White Background	Gray Background	Black Background	
				TINTS
				SATURATED COLORS
				SHADES
				MIXED VALUES
				MIXED VALUES

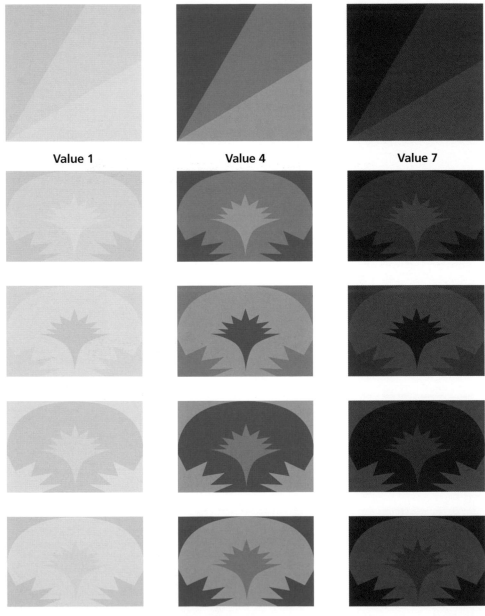

Value 1   Value 4   Value 7

RED/ORANGE, ORANGE AND YELLOW/ORANGE

No Background   White Background   Gray Background   Black Background

TINTS

SATURATED COLORS

SHADES

MIXED VALUES

MIXED VALUES

ANALOGOUS COMBINATIONS

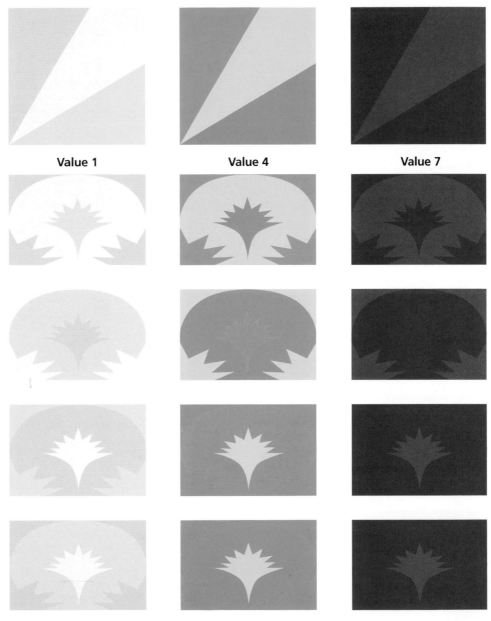

Value 1   Value 4   Value 7

No Background   White Background   Gray Background   Black Background

TINTS

SATURATED COLORS

SHADES

MIXED VALUES

MIXED VALUES

135

ANALOGOUS COMBINATIONS

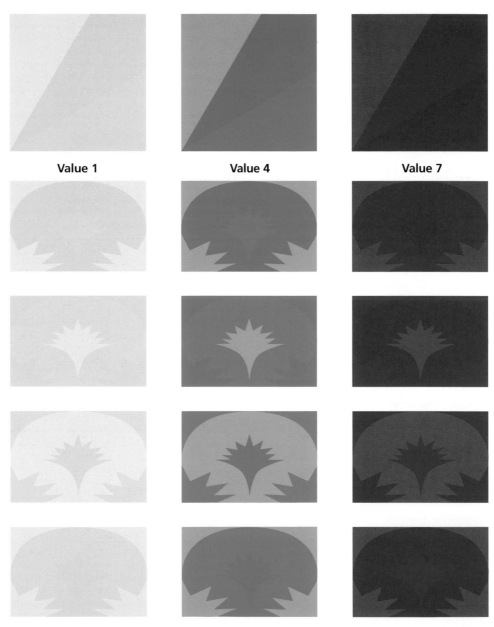

Value 1   Value 4   Value 7

YELLOW/GREEN, GREEN AND BLUE/GREEN

No Background
White Background
Gray Background
Black Background
TINTS
SATURATED COLORS
SHADES
MIXED VALUES
MIXED VALUES

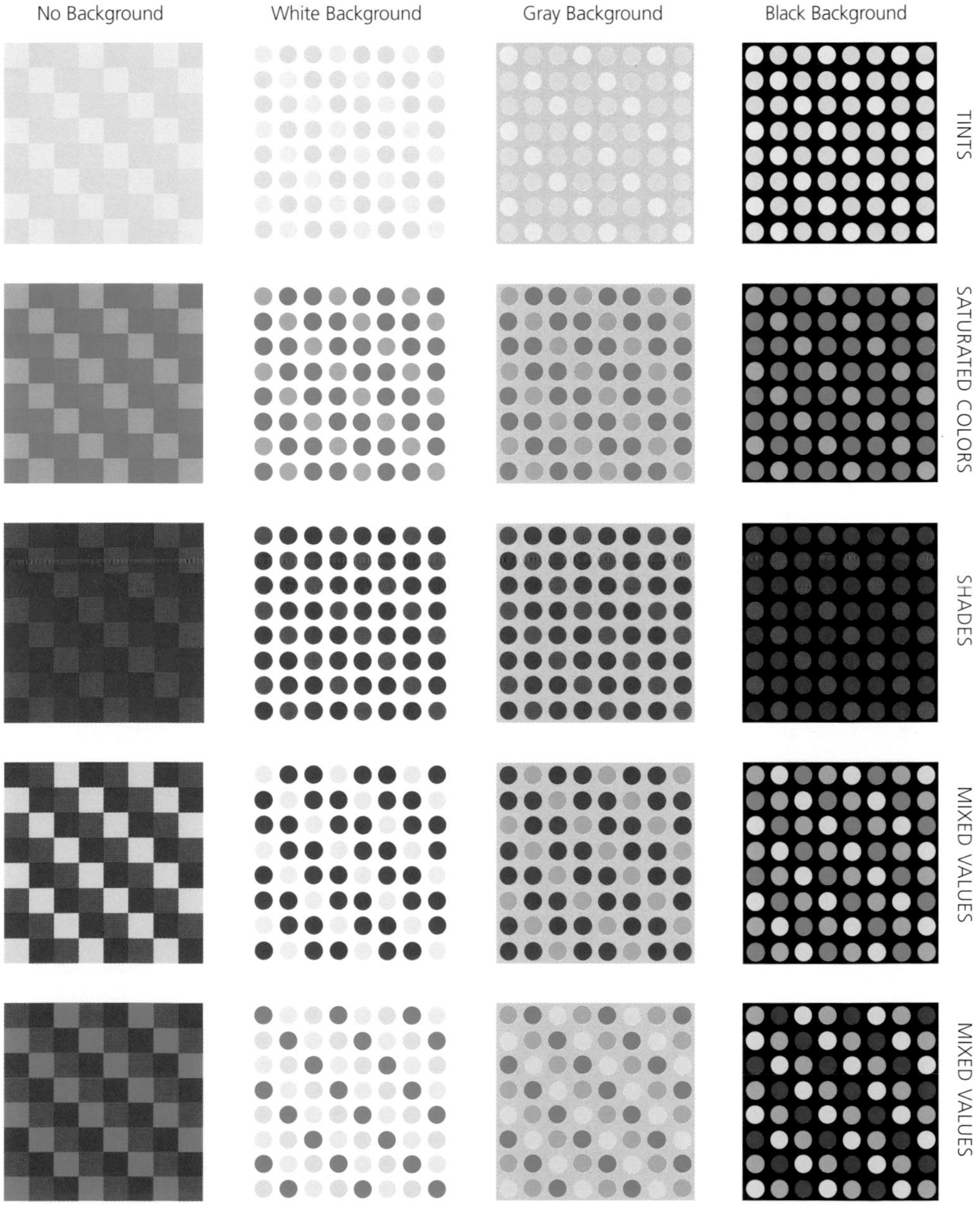

ANALOGOUS COMBINATIONS

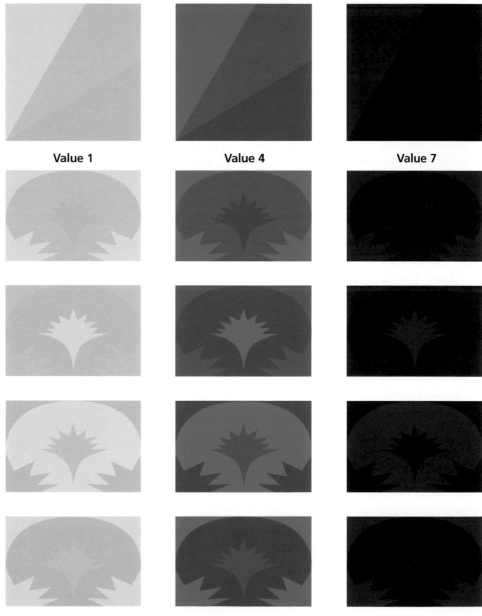

Value 1   Value 4   Value 7

BLUE/GREEN, BLUE AND BLUE/VIOLET

No Background	White Background	Gray Background	Black Background	
				TINTS
				SATURATED COLORS
				SHADES
				MIXED VALUES
				MIXED VALUES

139

Value 1　　　　Value 4　　　　Value 7

No Background   White Background   Gray Background   Black Background

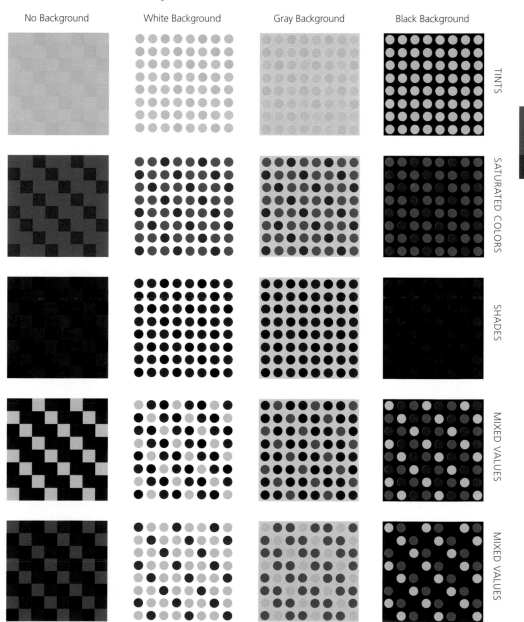

TINTS

SATURATED COLORS

SHADES

MIXED VALUES

MIXED VALUES

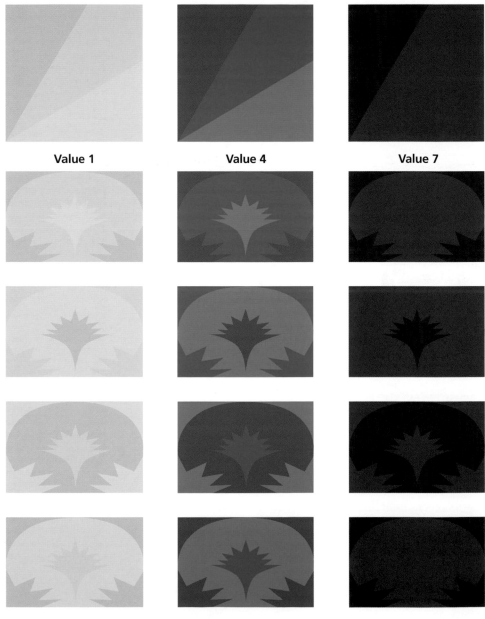

Value 1   Value 4   Value 7

RED/VIOLET, RED AND RED/ORANGE

No Background   White Background   Gray Background   Black Background

TINTS

SATURATED COLORS

SHADES

MIXED VALUES

MIXED VALUES

Four-Color Combinations

Tetrads are combinations that contain two pairs of complementary colors. When the complementary colors are equally spaced, they form a square tetrad. When the pairs of complements are separated by one color family, they form a rectangular tetrad. When they are next to each other, they are called double complements. Use the purple square on the inner wheel of the ColorSense Color Selector to find square tetrads and the green rectangle to find rectangular tetrads. Double complements are not represented by a symbol on the ColorSense Color Selector.

Although tetrads are among the most difficult combinations to work with because the colors are spaced around the color wheel, by making one color clearly dominant with the others as supporting or accent colors, you can create interesting and unusual combinations.

Square Tetrad

Double Complements

Rectangular Tetrad

Analogous Colors with Complement combinations are harmonious, like all analogous combinations, but have a spark of excitement provided by the addition of the complementary color. These combinations are not represented by a symbol on the ColorSense Color Selector.

Analogous Colors with Complement

SQUARE TETRADS

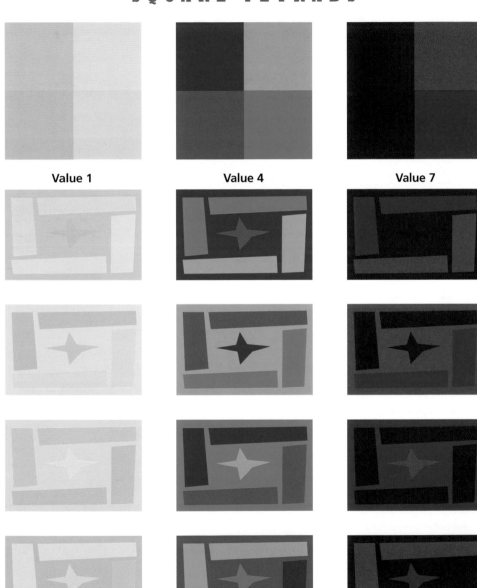

Value 1   Value 4   Value 7

146

RED, YELLOW/ORANGE, GREEN AND BLUE/VIOLET

No Background White Background Gray Background Black Background

TINTS

SATURATED COLORS

SHADES

MIXED VALUES

MIXED VALUES

SQUARE TETRADS

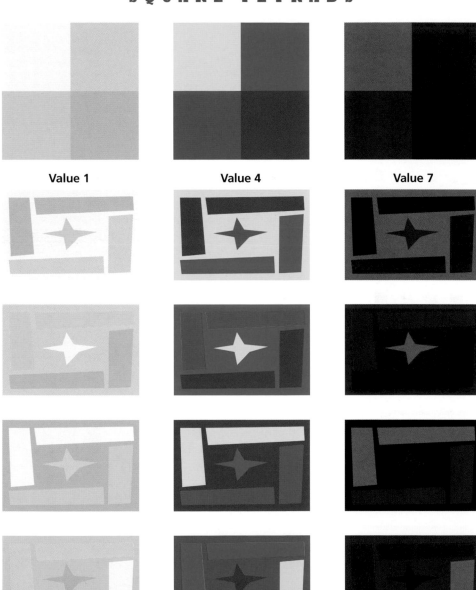

Value 1   Value 4   Value 7

No Background   White Background   Gray Background   Black Background

TINTS

SATURATED COLORS

SHADES

MIXED VALUES

MIXED VALUES

SQUARE TETRADS

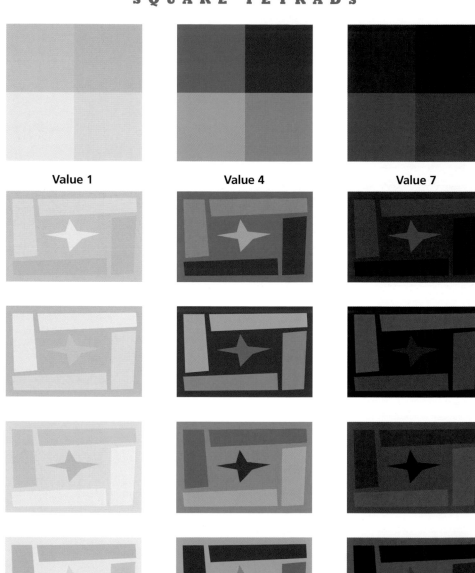

Value 1   Value 4   Value 7

BLUE, RED/VIOLET, ORANGE AND YELLOW/GREEN

No Background	White Background	Gray Background	Black Background	
				TINTS
				SATURATED COLORS
				SHADES
				MIXED VALUES
				MIXED VALUES

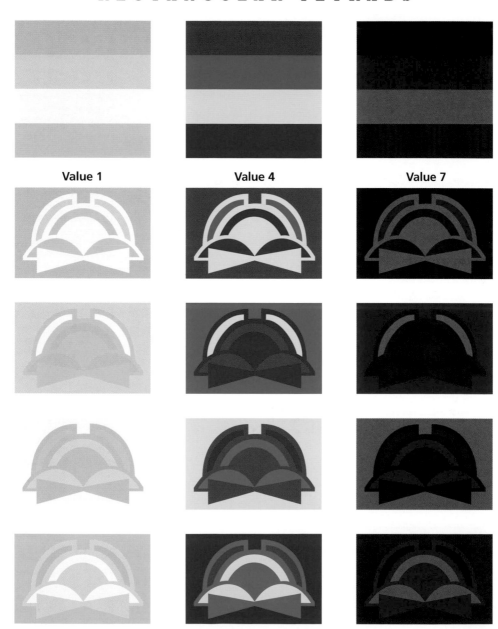

Value 1   Value 4   Value 7

RED, YELLOW, GREEN AND VIOLET

No Background	White Background	Gray Background	Black Background	

TINTS

SATURATED COLORS

SHADES

MIXED VALUES

MIXED VALUES

RECTANGULAR TETRADS

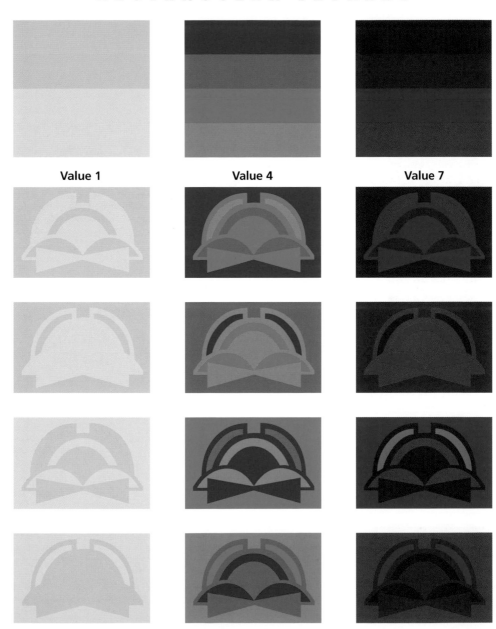

Value 1   Value 4   Value 7

ORANGE, GREEN, BLUE AND RED

No Background   White Background   Gray Background   Black Background

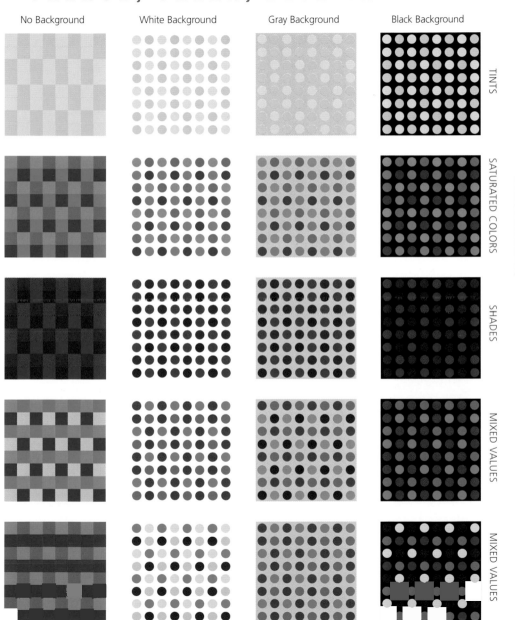

TINTS

SATURATED COLORS

SHADES

MIXED VALUES

MIXED VALUES

155

RECTANGULAR TETRADS

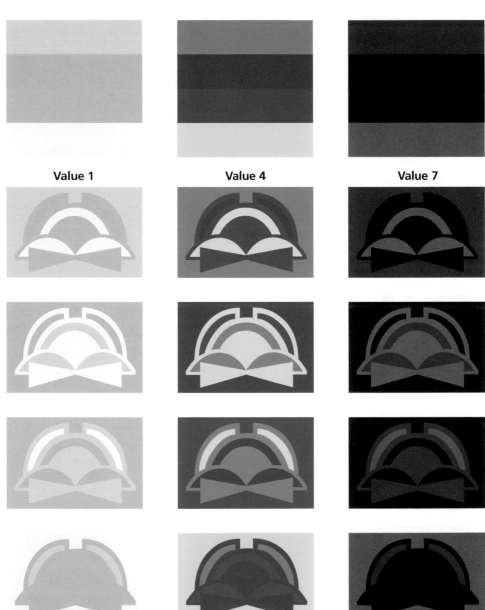

Value 1   Value 4   Value 7

No Background   White Background   Gray Background   Black Background

TINTS

SATURATED COLORS

SHADES

MIXED VALUES

MIXED VALUES

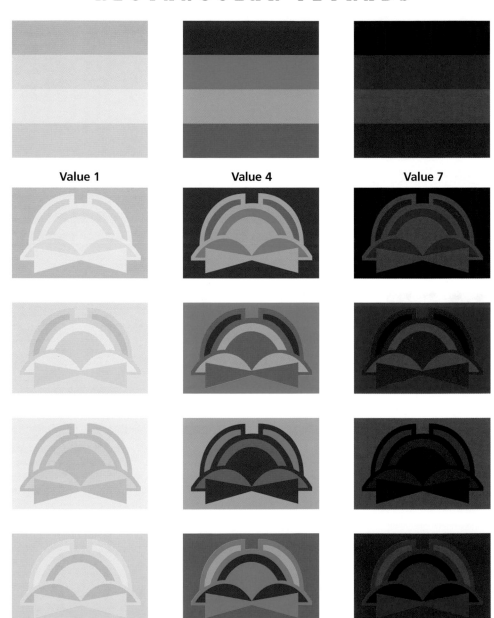

Value 1   Value 4   Value 7

RED/ORANGE, YELLOW/GREEN, BLUE/GREEN AND RED/VIOLET

No Background   White Background   Gray Background   Black Background

TINTS

SATURATED COLORS

SHADES

MIXED VALUES

MIXED VALUES

RECTANGULAR TETRADS

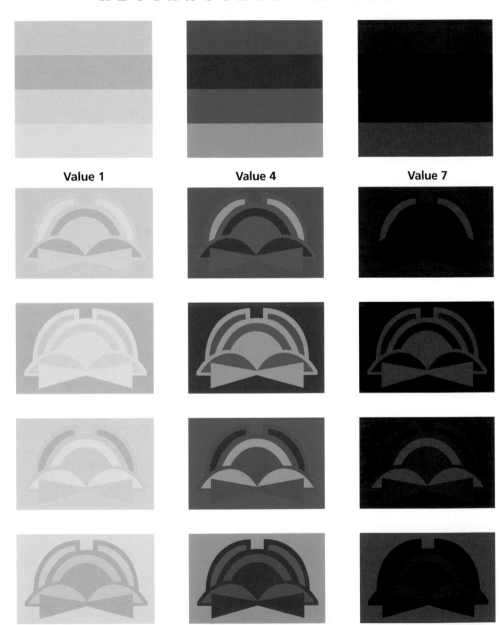

Value 1 Value 4 Value 7

No Background   White Background   Gray Background   Black Background

TINTS

SATURATED COLORS

SHADES

MIXED VALUES

MIXED VALUES

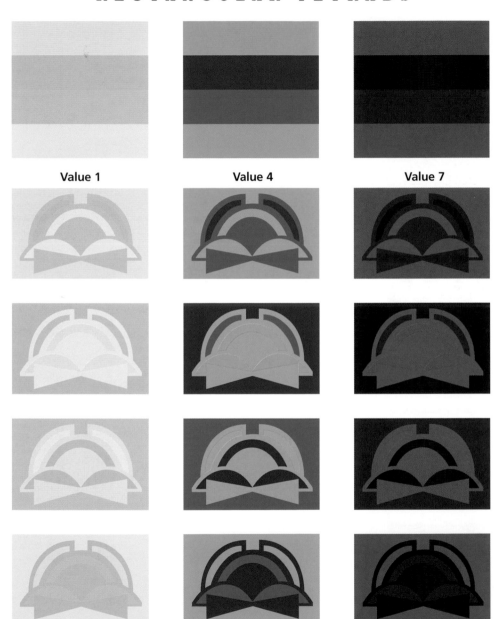

Value 1   Value 4   Value 7

YELLOW/GREEN, BLUE/VIOLET, RED/VIOLET AND YELLOW/ORANGE

No Background   White Background   Gray Background   Black Background

TINTS

SATURATED COLORS

SHADES

MIXED VALUES

MIXED VALUES

DOUBLE COMPLEMENTS

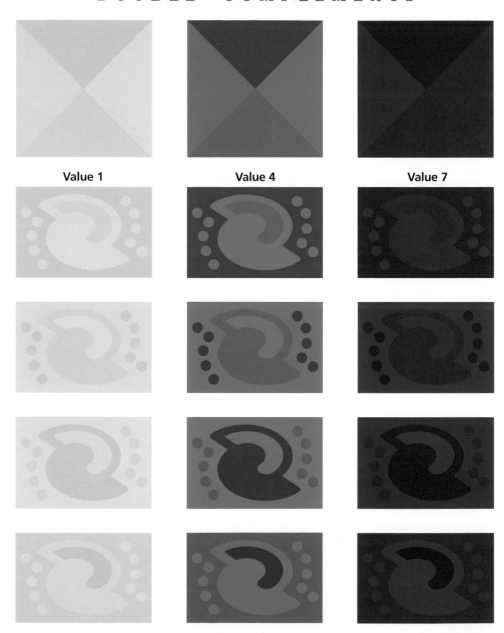

Value 1 Value 4 Value 7

RED, RED/ORANGE, GREEN AND BLUE/GREEN

No Background	White Background	Gray Background	Black Background	

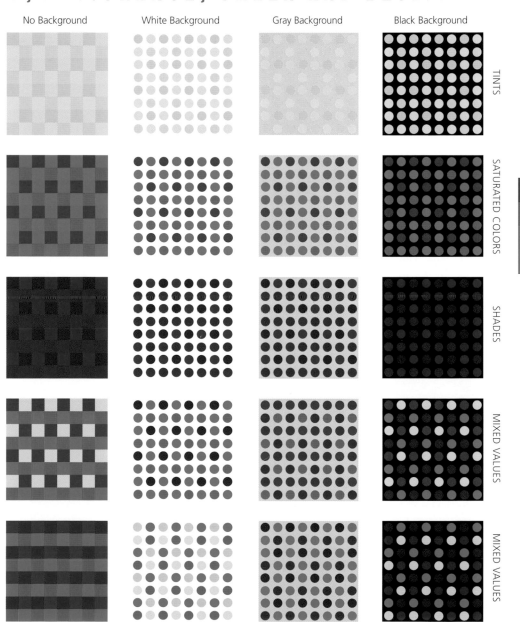

TINTS

SATURATED COLORS

SHADES

MIXED VALUES

MIXED VALUES

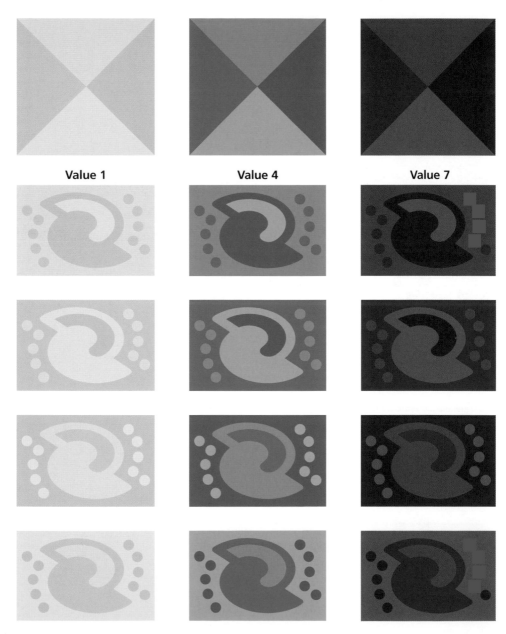

Value 1   Value 4   Value 7

No Background   White Background   Gray Background   Black Background

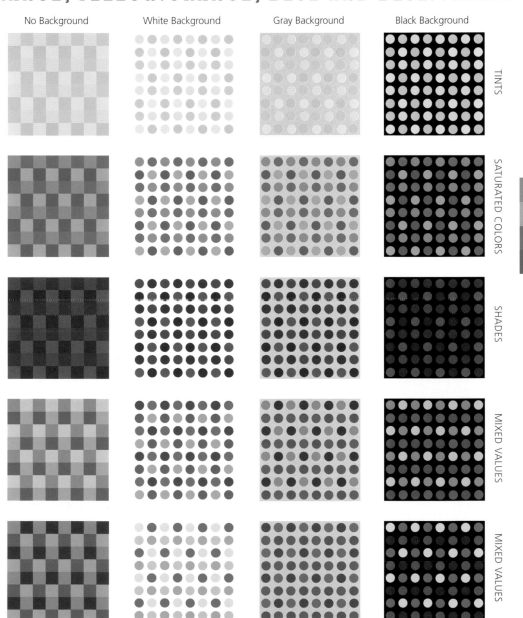

TINTS

SATURATED COLORS

SHADES

MIXED VALUES

MIXED VALUES

DOUBLE COMPLEMENTS

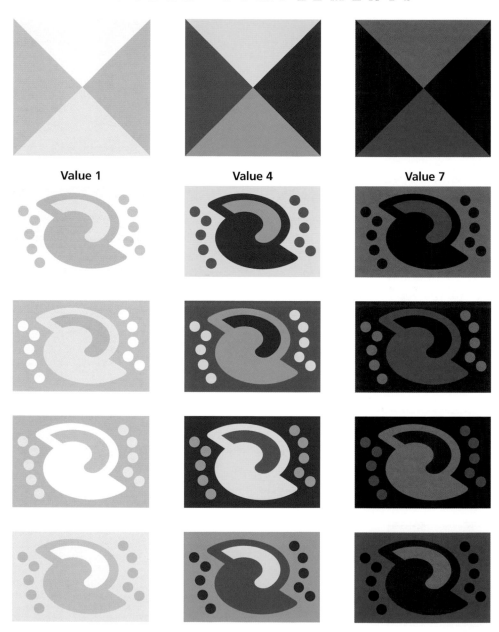

Value 1

Value 4

Value 7

YELLOW, YELLOW/GREEN, VIOLET AND RED/VIOLET

No Background	White Background	Gray Background	Black Background	
				TINTS
				SATURATED COLORS
				SHADES
				MIXED VALUES
				MIXED VALUES

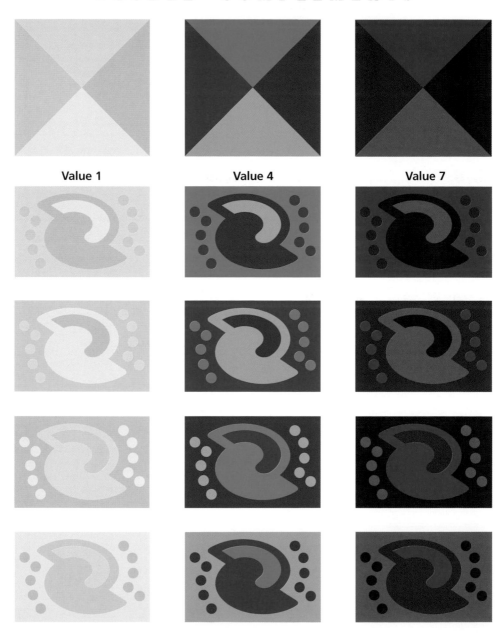

Value 1   Value 4   Value 7

No Background   White Background   Gray Background   Black Background

TINTS

SATURATED COLORS

SHADES

MIXED VALUES

MIXED VALUES

171

DOUBLE COMPLEMENTS

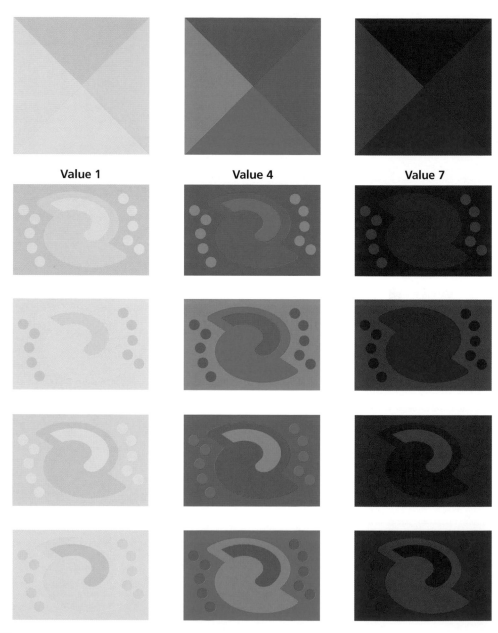

Value 1   Value 4   Value 7

172

No Background   White Background   Gray Background   Black Background

TINTS

SATURATED COLORS

SHADES

MIXED VALUES

MIXED VALUES

DOUBLE COMPLEMENTS

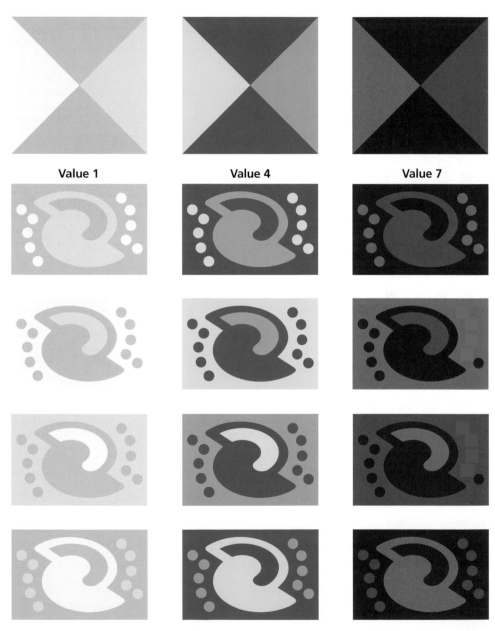

Value 1　　　　　Value 4　　　　　Value 7

VIOLET, BLUE/VIOLET, YELLOW AND YELLOW/ORANGE

No Background   White Background   Gray Background   Black Background

TINTS

SATURATED COLORS

SHADES

MIXED VALUES

MIXED VALUES

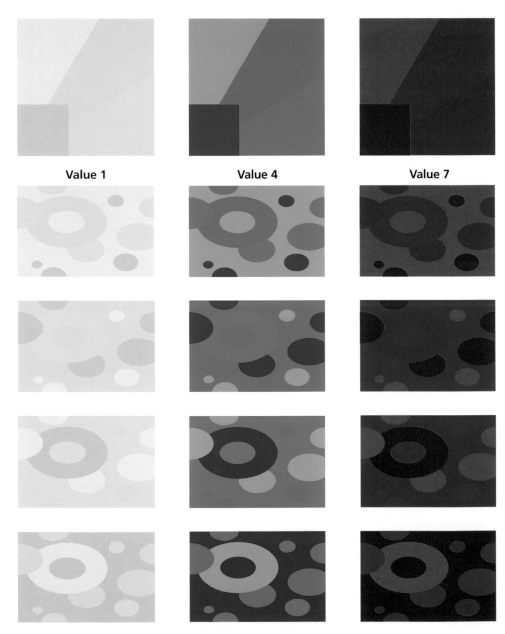

Value 1   Value 4   Value 7

No Background   White Background   Gray Background   Black Background

TINTS

SATURATED COLORS

SHADES

MIXED VALUES

MIXED VALUES

ANALOGOUS COLORS WITH COMPLEMENT

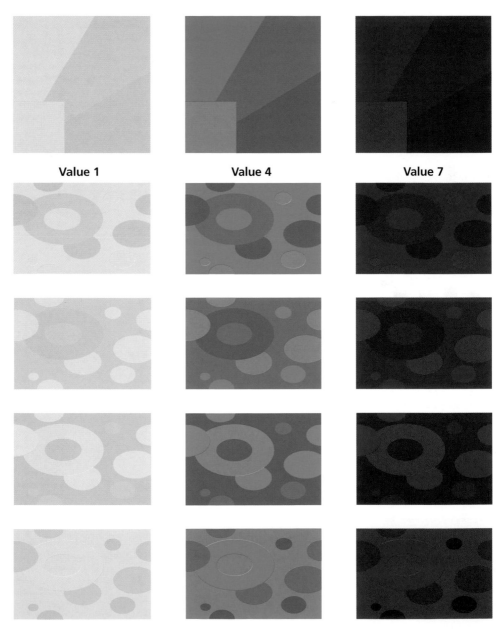

Value 1   Value 4   Value 7

No Background   White Background   Gray Background   Black Background

TINTS

SATURATED COLORS

SHADES

MIXED VALUES

MIXED VALUES

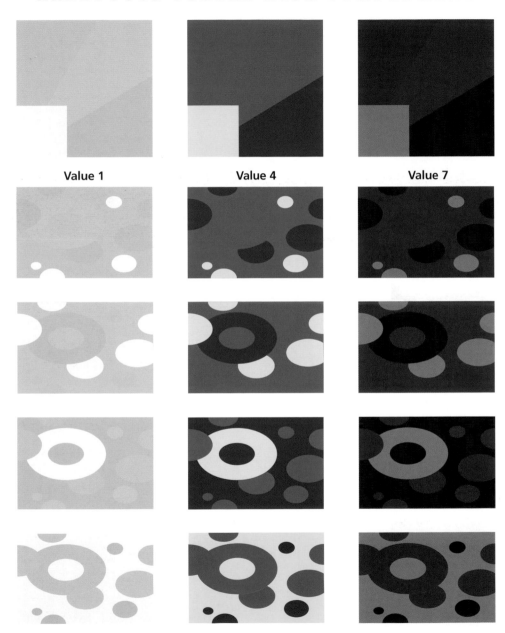

Value 1   Value 4   Value 7

No Background   White Background   Gray Background   Black Background

TINTS

SATURATED COLORS

SHADES

MIXED VALUES

MIXED VALUES

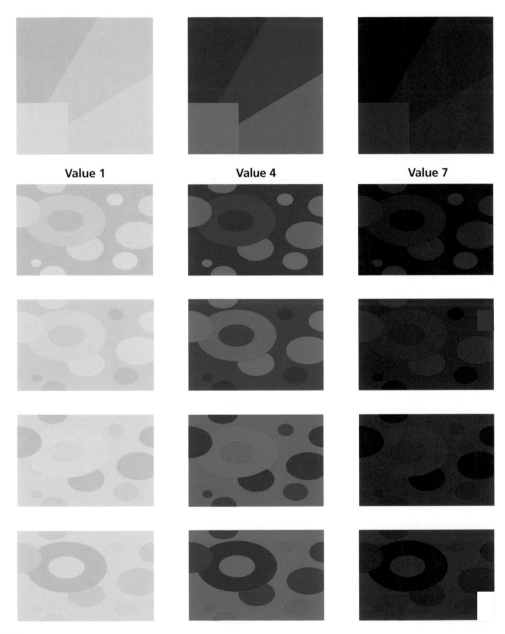

Value 1   Value 4   Value 7

No Background   White Background   Gray Background   Black Background

TINTS

SATURATED COLORS

SHADES

MIXED VALUES

MIXED VALUES

ANALOGOUS COLORS WITH COMPLEMENT

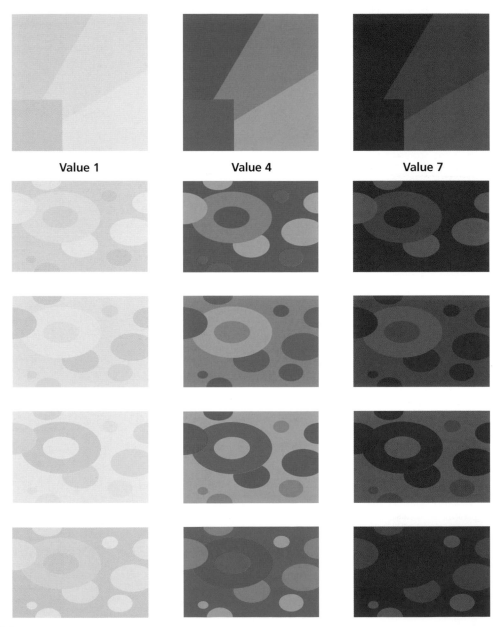

Value 1 Value 4 Value 7

RED/ORANGE, ORANGE, YELLOW/ORANGE AND BLUE

No Background   White Background   Gray Background   Black Background

TINTS

SATURATED COLORS

SHADES

MIXED VALUES

MIXED VALUES

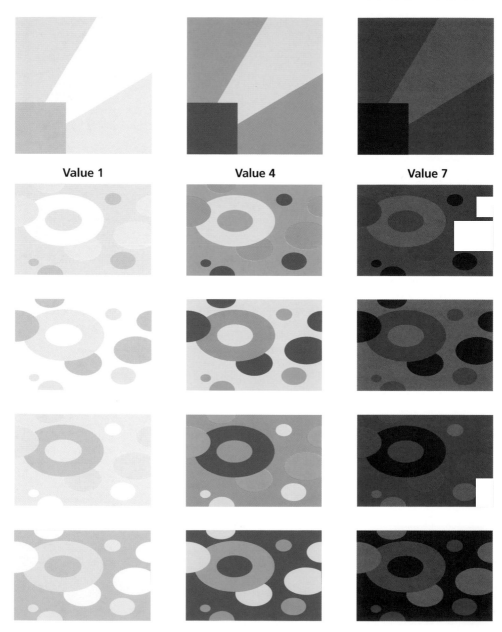

Value 1

Value 4

Value 7

YELLOW/ORANGE, YELLOW, YELLOW/GREEN AND VIOLET

No Background   White Background   Gray Background   Black Background

TINTS

SATURATED COLORS

SHADES

MIXED VALUES

MIXED VALUES

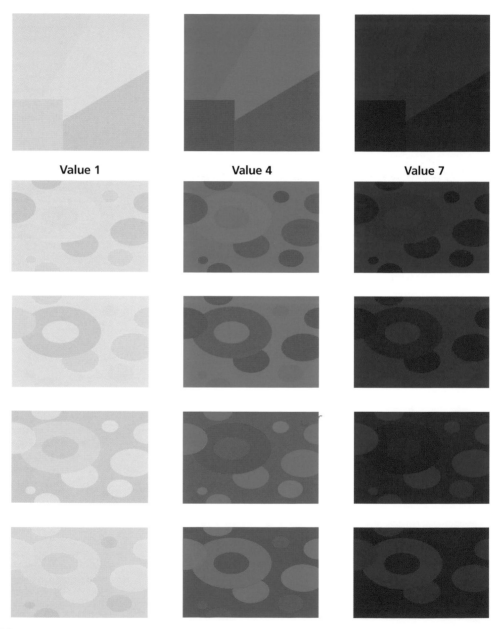

Value 1   Value 4   Value 7

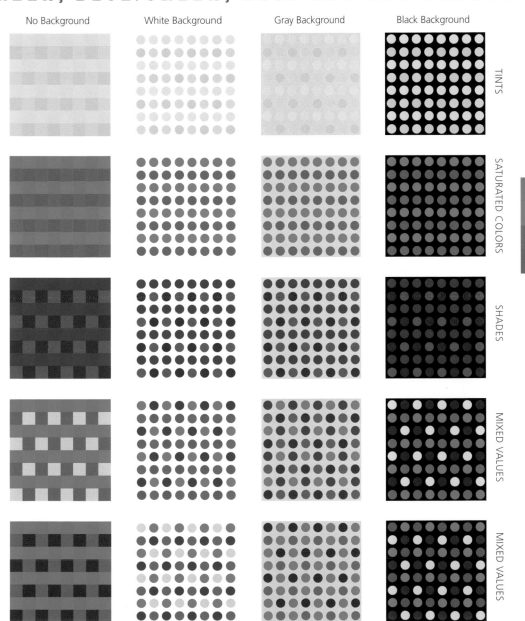

No Background   White Background   Gray Background   Black Background

TINTS

SATURATED COLORS

SHADES

MIXED VALUES

MIXED VALUES

189

ANALOGOUS COLORS WITH COMPLEMENT

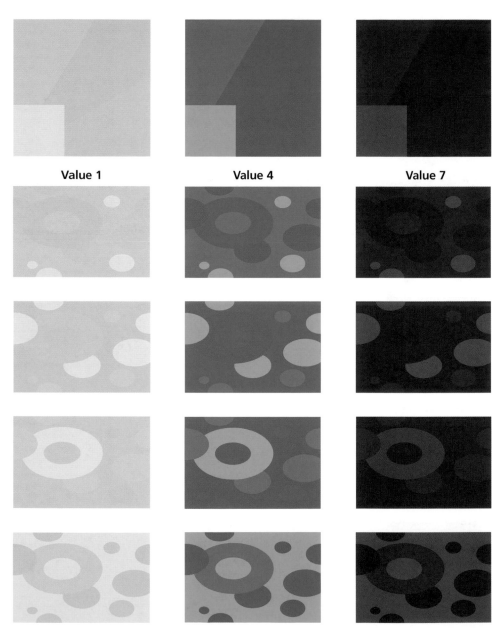

Value 1   Value 4   Value 7

BLUE, BLUE/VIOLET, VIOLET AND YELLOW/ORANGE

No Background   White Background   Gray Background   Black Background

TINTS

SATURATED COLORS

SHADES

MIXED VALUES

MIXED VALUES

ANALOGOUS COLORS WITH COMPLEMENT

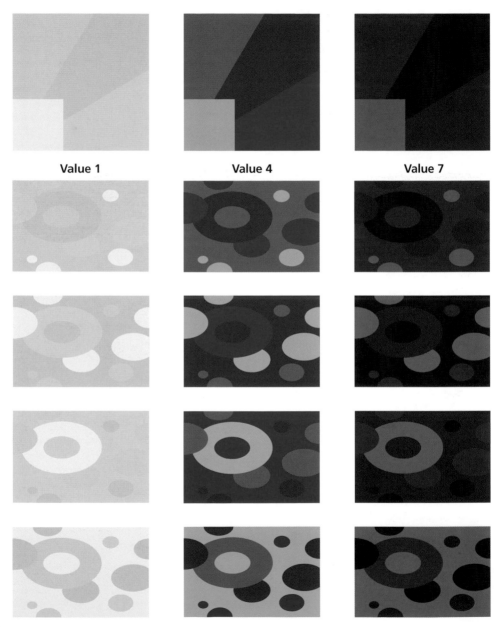

Value 1   Value 4   Value 7

No Background   White Background   Gray Background   Black Background

TINTS

SATURATED COLORS

SHADES

MIXED VALUES

MIXED VALUES

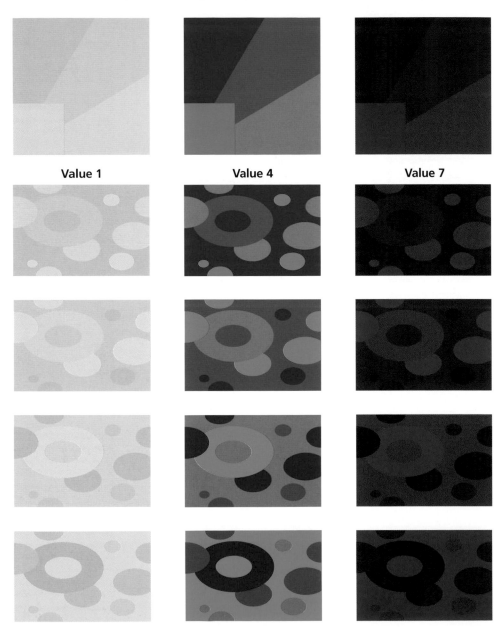

Value 1   Value 4   Value 7

RED, RED/ORANGE, ORANGE AND BLUE/GREEN

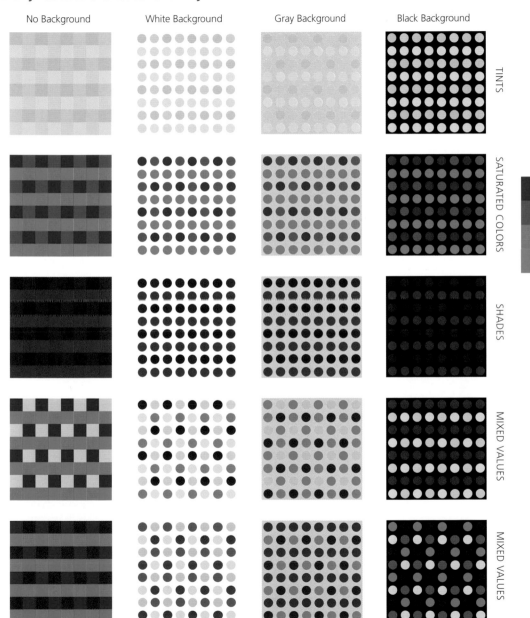

No Background White Background Gray Background Black Background

TINTS

SATURATED COLORS

SHADES

MIXED VALUES

MIXED VALUES

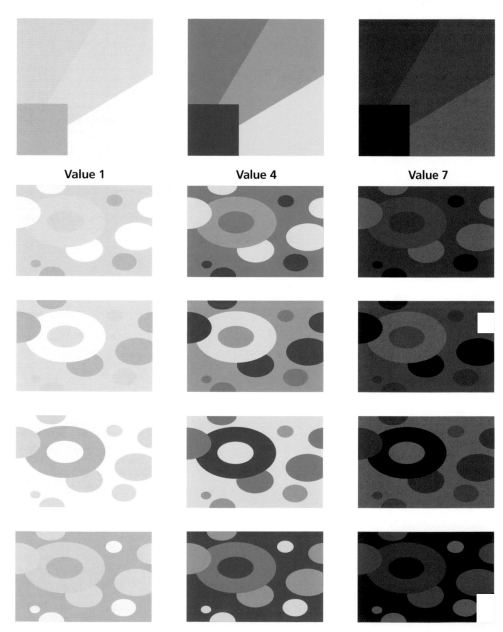

Value 1 Value 4 Value 7

No Background   White Background   Gray Background   Black Background

TINTS

SATURATED COLORS

SHADES

MIXED VALUES

MIXED VALUES

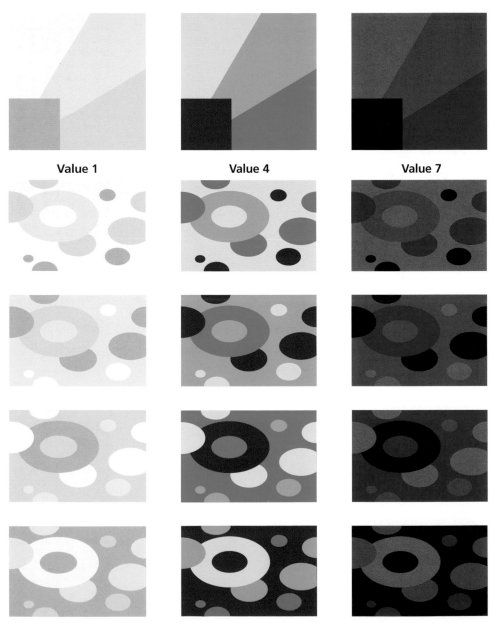

Value 1   Value 4   Value 7

No Background   White Background   Gray Background   Black Background

TINTS

SATURATED COLORS

SHADES

MIXED VALUES

MIXED VALUES

INDEX OF COLORS

	Monochromatic Combinations	Two-Color Combinations	Three-Color Combinations	Four-Color Combinations
Red	24	50, 62, 64	88, 96, 98, 114, 120, 130, 142	146, 152, 154, 164, 170, 176, 182, 192, 194
Red/Orange	26	56, 76, 78	94, 104, 108, 110, 120, 132, 142	148, 158, 160, 164, 172, 182, 184, 188, 194
Orange	28	52, 66, 68	90, 98, 100, 116, 120, 122, 132	150, 154, 156, 166, 172, 178, 184, 194, 196
Yellow/Orange	30	58, 80, 82	92, 106, 110, 112, 122, 132, 134	146, 160, 162, 166, 174, 184, 186, 190, 196
Yellow	32	54, 70, 72	88, 100, 102, 118, 122, 124, 134	148, 152, 156, 168, 174, 180, 186, 196, 198
Yellow/Green	34	60, 62, 84	94, 96, 112, 114, 124, 134, 136	150, 158, 162, 168, 170, 176, 186, 192, 198
Green	36	50, 74, 76	90, 102, 104, 108, 124, 126, 136	146, 152, 154, 164, 170, 176, 182, 188, 198
Blue/Green	38	56, 64, 66	92, 98, 114, 116, 126, 136, 138	148, 158, 160, 164, 172, 176, 178, 188, 194
Blue	40	52, 78, 80	88, 104, 106, 110, 126, 128, 138	150, 154, 156, 166, 172, 178, 184, 188, 190
Blue/Violet	42	58, 68, 70	94, 100, 116, 118, 128, 138, 140	146, 160, 162, 166, 174, 178, 180, 190, 196
Violet	44	54, 82, 84	90, 96, 106, 112, 128, 130, 140	148, 152, 156, 168, 174, 180, 186, 190, 192
Red/Violet	46	60, 72, 74	92, 102, 108, 118, 130, 140, 142	150, 158, 162, 168, 170, 180, 182, 192, 198

PHOTO CREDITS:
Michael Kraus: Cover, pp. 2–3
Jack Deutsch Studio: pp. 1, 7, 12–13, 20, 49, 87, 145
Marie-Claire: p. 23

Classic Red #1 Ballerina	Classic Red #2 Pink Carnation	Classic Red #3 Geranium
Classic Red #4 Crimson	Classic Red #5 Poinsettia	Classic Red #6 Ruby
Classic Red #7 Garnet	White	Black

Classic Red/Orange #1 Peach	Classic Red/Orange #2 Shrimp	Classic Red/Orange #3 Coral
Classic Red/Orange #4 Pimento	Classic Red/Orange #5 Paprika	Classic Red/Orange #6 Tabasco
Classic Red/Orange #7 Cinnamon	White	Gray #7

Classic Orange #1
Mimosa

Classic Orange #2
Creamsicle

Classic Orange #3
Cantaloupe

Classic Orange #4
Tangerine

Classic Orange #5
Sweet Potato

Classic Orange #6
Saddle

Classic Orange #7
Cola

White

Gray #6

Classic Yellow/Orange #1 Nectar	Classic Yellow/Orange #2 Honey	Classic Yellow/Orange #3 Marmalade
Classic Yellow/Orange #4 Squash	Classic Yellow/Orange #5 Peanut	Classic Yellow/Orange #6 Gingersnap
Classic Yellow/Orange #7 Fudge	White	Gray #5

Classic Yellow #1
Meringue

Classic Yellow #2
Lemonade

Classic Yellow #3
Banana

Classic Yellow #4
Sunshine

Classic Yellow #5
Pineapple

Classic Yellow #6
Curry

Classic Yellow #7
Chutney

White

Gray #4

Classic Yellow/Green #1 Celery	Classic Yellow/Green #2 Lettuce	Classic Yellow/Green #3 Lime
Classic Yellow/Green #4 New Grass	Classic Yellow/Green #5 Parsley	Classic Yellow/Green #6 Pine
Classic Yellow/Green #7 Army	White	Gray #3

Classic Green #1
Honey Dew

Classic Green #2
Spearmint

Classic Green #3
Clover

Classic Green #4
Kelly

Classic Green #5
Forest

Classic Green #6
Timberline

Classic Green #7
Cypress

White

Gray #2

Classic Blue/Green #1
Seafoam

Classic Blue/Green #2
Oasis

Classic Blue/Green #3
Aqua

Classic Blue/Green #4
Peacock

Classic Blue/Green #5
Caribbean

Classic Blue/Green #6
Lagoon

Classic Blue/Green #7
Baltic

White

Gray #1

Classic Blue #1
Ice Cube

Classic Blue #2
Sky

Classic Blue #3
Cornflower

Classic Blue #4
Delft

Classic Blue #5
Sapphire

Classic Blue #6
Seaport

Classic Blue #7
Deep Sea

White

White

Classic Blue/Violet #1
Surf

Classic Blue/Violet #2
Cerulean

Classic Blue/Violet #3
Morning Glory

Classic Blue/Violet #4
Periwinkle

Classic Blue/Violet #5
Blueprint

Classic Blue/Violet #6
Ocean Storm

Classic Blue/Violet #7
Midnight

White

White

Classic Violet #1
Lilac

Classic Violet #2
Heliotrope

Classic Violet #3
African Violet

Classic Violet #4
Violetta

Classic Violet #5
Mulberry

Classic Violet #6
Grape

Classic Violet #7
Eggplant

White

White

Classic Red/Violet #1
Rosebud

Classic Red/Violet #2
Rouge

Classic Red/Violet #3
Rhododendron

Classic Red/Violet #4
Magenta

Classic Red/Violet #5
Beet

Classic Red/Violet #6
Merlot

Classic Red/Violet #7
Black Cherry

White

White

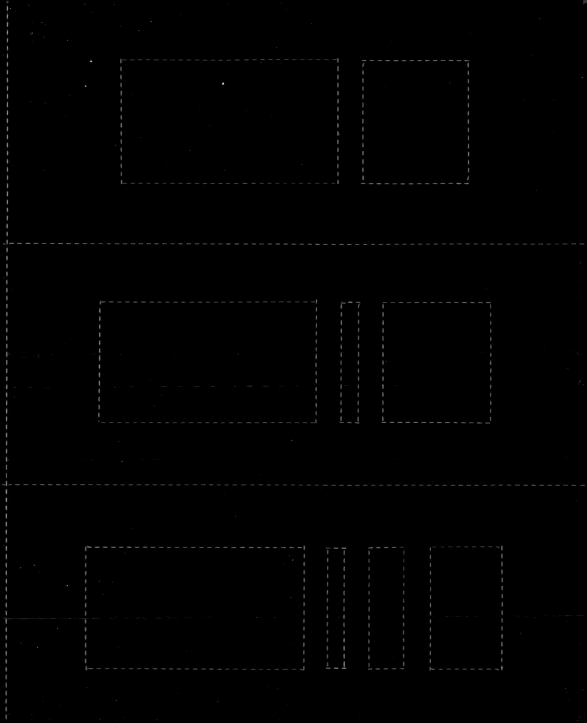